DIVORCE

(STEP BY STEP GUIDE)

DASA

There are many books and essays treating all legal subjects from a theory point of view. Dealing with everything from basic explanations of the system to erudite academic discussions of obscure points. These are the best left to the academics, their students, and the practicing profession. The theoretical discussions will not sell well to the lay public.

There are any numbers of self-help books on the market. They deal with explanations of the legal system, as a system, sometimes give advice, but they are still general advice books.

The legal document publishing companies make their forms available in blank. Virtually no guidance is provided with the blank forms and the lay publics are entirely on their own.

Paralegals have entered to help give general advice at a nominal cost but few are capable and knowledgeable. As it stands now, they are regulated by the Law Society in many Provinces and States and quite possibly regulated out of business.

The idea of this KIT is to make it a short, plain language explanation telling the lay individual exactly how to go about getting a divorce which will include the legal **documents and forms**, already filled out *pro forma*, to do just that.

Included will be specific individual examples of how to get the desired divorce for each one of the most common fact situations. Any lay individual can then simply look up his/her specific situation and follow the step by step procedure, using the given examples, to achieve the desired goal.

A Separation Agreement is an integral part of any divorce and will include a division of assets. This kit contains a detailed separation agreement to help with your divorce.

Included to help the divorcing parent will be a **Parenting Guide** for instructional, reference and educational use. It could be used by parents working together on a Parenting agreement or method to negotiate access and custody arrangements.

All items will give you a comprehensive view of most things necessary to complete your divorce.

1. LEGAL PROVISIONS

So you have finally come to the point where you are thinking about a divorce. But can you? Are you eligible? Are you prepared? Are you sure you know where you stand in terms of your legal rights and obligations? These are the basic questions that you must determine. This book will try to guide you on the basics in plain language. Then, once you have determined that you are ready to go ahead, this book will try to guide you on how to go about it, again in simple, plain language.

So, here we go. First, the essentials in brief of the legal scene in North America regarding divorce

Who may apply for a divorce? Are you eligible? Throughout North America nearly anyone who is legally married can apply for a divorce. There are, however, a few criteria that must be satisfied before a North American court will hear a divorce application. The criteria that you must satisfy are:

I That you have legal status:

- Recognized marriage;
- Recognized residence;
- Competence.

II. That you have grounds (an acceptable reason) for divorce, including proof.

A. LEGAL STATUS

(i) Recognized Marriage

In order to apply for a divorce one must first be married. Seem obvious? Well, don't be so sure.

If your marriage (1) took place in North America and (2) was presided over by a licensed clergy person, Justice of the Peace or Judge, there is likely no problem. You are considered legally married. But if your marriage ceremony was performed in another country, this could be a problem. The foreign form of marriage ceremony will be recognized in a North American jurisdiction if it conforms to the same legal standards and requirements as a North American marriage ceremony. Note that this has nothing to do with religious rituals or beliefs. It is the legal form of the ceremony that is relevant to divorce court.

Here are the qualifying criteria:

- The marriage ceremony must have been presided over by a cleric or civil official who was licensed to perform weddings;
- You and your spouse must have been residents in the country or jurisdiction where the ceremony took place for at least one year*
- The form of marriage ceremony must have been recognized as legally valid in the foreign country or jurisdiction where it was performed;
- You and your spouse must have been of legal age to marry at the time you married (usually 16);
- You and your spouse must have been mentally competent (of legally sound mind) at the time youmarried;
- You and your spouse must have lived together openly and publicly as man and wife and been regarded generally as man and wife in the foreign community;
- You and your spouse must have no others that either of you regard as a spouse simultaneously to your

marriage together (i.e., no polygamous relationships).

- This particular criterion is known to be treated somewhat flexibly by the courts and by immigration authorities from time to time, so if you got married on a trip it does not automatically invalidate your marriage, you just may have a harder time having it recognized.

Of course, having a marriage certificate issued by the relevant foreign government authority, and an English translation of it, certified by the translator for accuracy, helps greatly to overcome most obstacles. Many jurisdictions make this compulsory

If there is any doubt whatever as to the legal validity of the marriage ceremony, an almost sure solution to the problem is to go to a lawyer and pay for an opinion letter stating that the lawyer has inquired into the form of the foreign marriage ceremony and found it to be legally valid and acceptable in your jurisdiction in North America. If a lawyer is unwilling or unable to sign such a letter, your only alternative, other than consulting another lawyer, is to seek a divorce in the country or jurisdiction where the marriage took place.

(ii) Residence Requirement.

Most North American jurisdictions require that you are a resident of the state or province in which you want to apply for divorce for at least one year before you apply. The notable exception to this rule is the State of Nevada, where you must reside for one week before you are eligible for a divorce. But before you get the idea to go running off to Reno or Las Vegas for a gambling holiday and a quickie divorce, please note that these quickie divorces are not recognized anywhere in Canada and are recognized only in some of the states of the United States. The same recognition problem also exists with the so-called Mexican quickie divorces.

(iii) Mental Competence.

For the purpose of getting married the legal definition of mental competence is that a person can understand and appreciate the nature and consequences of the act of going through a marriage ceremony and getting married. For the purpose of getting divorced the definition of mental competence is that a person applying for a divorce or agreeing to a divorce can understand and appreciate the nature and consequences of applying for a divorce and getting divorced.

Can a person with a mental affliction get married? Can a person who is mentally challenged? Can such a person apply for a divorce, or agree to a divorce, or be served with divorce documents? In all these cases the answer is yes, as long as they can appreciate what a marriage is, what a divorce is, and the consequences.

B. GROUNDS FOR DIVORCE IN CANADA

(i) Marriage Breakdown.

If the marriage relationship, both physical and day-to-day living, has completely stopped, so that the spouses are living two separate, independent lives and conducting themselves as if they were single individuals, and if this has been going on for at least one year immediately prior, there is grounds for divorce. Usually there must be at least one year of continuously living at separate residences, but the law does allow the separation to be interrupted by a trial reconciliation. If the reconciliation continues for ninety consecutive days the couple is presumed to be fully reconciled. Then if the couple separates again the one year time requirement starts running all over again from zero.

(ii) Adultery.

If there is clear, indisputable evidence of one spouse's adultery then the other spouse has immediate grounds for divorce. Clear evidence would consist of clear, graphic compromising photographs of the spouse in the act of adultery, an admission of adultery by the spouse or another participant in the adultery (usually called the Co-Respondent), testimony by someone who observed the adultery, or circumstantial evidence of adultery so clear and beyond question that there is no room for doubt in the mind of the judge. All direct evidence and testimony must be supported by a corroborative witness; that is, a second, independent person with direct knowledge of the adultery, who can swear to the fact that the allegations of adultery are true and accurate.

Care must be taken to satisfy the judge that the applicant spouse has not forgiven (condoned) the respondent spouse for the act or acts of adultery. Condoning the adultery would mean the adultery is no longer grounds for divorce.

(iii) Cruelty.

Most North American jurisdictions accept either physical or mental cruelty as grounds/or immediate divorce. Whether the specific acts of cruelty have a physical or mental effect, the cruelty must be so severe that continued marriage is absolutely intolerable to the spouse applying/or the divorce. This usually means that supporting corroborative medical evidence from a psychiatrist or psychologist is required to convince the judge that the marriage relationship is intolerable and cruel.

The legal definition of mental cruelty is spousal conduct creating an environment that threatens the psychological or emotional health of the applicant spouse to such a degree that it is intolerable for the applicant spouse to continue in the marriage relationship. The actual standard of conduct required for mental cruelty varies somewhat from jurisdiction to jurisdiction and from case to case but the most popular interpretation is that continuing in the marriage relationship is so completely repulsive that the very idea of continuing causes psychological or emotional damage and that the applicant for divorce can not now and will not in the future be able to function in daily married life. The implication that the judge must believe is that continued marriage would place the applicant for divorce in need of a significant amount of restorative medical care.

The legal definition of physical cruelty is slightly simpler. It means the applicant spouse has suffered at least one assault at the hands of the respondent spouse. It can also mean that there is a real and imminent fear or threat of an assault in the near future. The evidence of the past assault, pattern of assaults or the perceived threat of imminent assault must be documented, observable, and clear enough that it is convincing to the judge, or else it will not be acceptable. A corroborative independent witness and/or medical or police evidence is almost always required.

There is no ground for divorce by reason of cruelty when the act of cruelty complained of has been condoned (i.e., pardoned or forgiven) by the applicant spouse. That is why the standard application for divorce contains a statement certifying that there has been no condemnation of any act complained of in the application by the applicant.

(iv) Alcoholism or Substance Abuse.

Alcoholism or substance abuse (drug addiction) are NOT grounds for divorce, although some people are of the mistaken opinion they are. I know of no jurisdiction anywhere in North America where they are grounds for divorce.

The only way alcoholism or substance abuse could be relevant in a divorce application would be either as a cause for initiating separate residences, leading to marriage breakdown, or as evidence of behavior leading to an incident or incidents of such cruelty as to make the continued marriage intolerable. In either of these situations, the burden of providing convincing proof would apply as usual, as described above

Note the psychological or emotional factor in the cruelty ground. So is the imminent threat of a repeat of the act(s) of cruelty. They contribute to the next essential factor of cruelty, intolerability. These are essential parts of the cruelty ground, and if an applicant would try to allege an assault or a threat of intimidation without alleging the mental effects and without alleging that continuing would be intolerable, it is unlikely that the divorce application would be successful. Proving convincingly the mental element of cruelty is very difficult because convincing a judge of one's state of mind is very difficult. Therefore the cruelty ground is not often used in reality, in spite of all that we now know about how common spousal abuse is.

The most frequently used ground for divorce is marriage breakdown for one year or more. The second most popular ground is adultery. The person seeking the least complicated and most likely to succeed path to divorce should focus their attention on these.

Now, if you have decided whether you qualify for the divorce you want, and if you do, it is time to get prepared. Chapter 2 deals with Getting Prepared.

Divorce readiness - Getting Prepared

2. GETTING PREPARED

(i) Checklist of Your Divorce Readiness

The questions that follow are only guidelines, but if the answer to any of them is negative, you should not consider yourself ready to proceed yet.

1. If you do not yet live in your own separate residence, have you selected one, is it comfortable and affordable, and when are you prepared to move into it?
2. What is your ground for divorce?
3. Marriage Breakdown and separate residences for at least 1 year
   i. Adultery
   ii. Physical Cruelty
   iii. Mental Cruelty
   iv. What are the key facts? ____

   ____

   ____
5. Do you have the respondent spouse's correct date of birth and current address for service?
6. Do you have the correct name and address for service of the co-respondent, if any?
7. Have you got at least the tacit agreement of the respondent spouse and any co-respondent to cooperate with the intended procedure? (An argument or dispute adds drastically to the difficulty, delay, and cost of a divorce proceeding. Get as much cooperation as possible.)
8. Are any minor children prepared to say they are satisfied with custody and visiting arrangements affecting them, when officials ask them? (Children, especially younger ones, should be prepared gently and gradually for coming events, not shocked and surprised. It is important to let them know that the divorce is in no way their fault.
9. Do you know the address of your local court office, including street address, room number, zip or postal code and telephone number? (Yes, you will need this much detail.)
10. Do you know what expenses you will pay, including:
    - certified copy of marriage certificate *(.if you can't find your original)*
    - initial filing fee
    - process server's fee to serve documents
    - fee for the Official Guardian of Children or Children's Aid Society, where custody of minor children is an issue
    - record closing/setting down for trial fee *(exact name varies with jurisdiction)*
    - process server's fee for serving Decree Nisi *(.where applicable)*
    - application fee for Decree Absolute

To be safe you should allow about $500.00 for expenses.

2. Checklist of Legal Documents and Proof Required

Do you have:

a.) Your Marriage Certificate?

b.) If there was more than one marriage, your previous Marriage Certificates and Divorce Orders/Certificates?

c.) c)If there are children or adopted children of the current marriage, their birth certificates?

d.) If there are any minor or dependent children of this marriage, any Orders affecting their custody or financial support?

e.) A blank form of application or petition for divorce, as used in your jurisdiction? *(Can often be obtained from. local government web sites, local legal aid associations, legal help clinics, some generous minded law firms, believe it or not, and legal forms publishers.)*

f.) Document evidence/photos are you relying on? Describe:____________________________________

g.) Your principal witness for court? ____

h.) Is your principal witness a close friend or relative (not good) or an independent person (good)?*

i.) Who is your corroborative (second) witness for court? ___________________________________

j.) Is your corroborative witness a close friend or relative (not good) or an independent person (good)?

**Note: Many divorce applicants are their own principal witness. This is okay. You are prejudiced in your own favour. You can't help it. That is why judges routinely require a second, corroborative witness, who is independent, without anything to gain or lose in the divorce. If you can manage it, an independent primary witness is a good idea. Independent principal and corroborative witnesses give you the advantage of two unbiased proofs of your allegations, two opportunities to convince the judge you deserve what you ask for. If the grounds are more difficult to prove, such as adultery or cruelty, two independent witnesses to support your claims may be more than just a good idea, they may be essential.*

3 Checklist for Financial Issues

Do you have:

1. Financial statement forms, of income and living expenses, and of assets and liabilities, in the correct form for your jurisdiction, if financial support is to be an issue in your divorce application?
2. An added up calculation of what your monthly income and expenses are?
3. A firm idea of by how much you are breaking even or not breaking even?
4. Calculations showing how much, if anything, do you need *(not want, NEED)* in financial support to get by?
5. Clear and up-to-date knowledge of what the respondent spouse's income and monthly living expenses are? What is the respondent's net disposable *(surplus)* income?
6. Clear calculations showing what the respondent spouse realistically can afford to pay and why?
7. A list of the assets of the marriage? A list of who wants what? A document of mutual agreement as to what division has been agreed to?
8. A list of what financial claims and loans there are secured against the assets? A list of how much the payments per month are against each? A document of mutual agreement as to which spouse can afford to make which of the necessary payments?
9. If an asset is to be sold, a calculation of how much money there will be to divide after payment of all financial debts connected with it?
10. ll life insurance policies you are interested in? What is their monthly/annual payment? What is the equity *(cash surrender)* value? Who is the named beneficiary? After divorce, who will make the premium payments? Who will be the beneficiary? Is the beneficiary irrevocable *(unchangeable)?*
11. How much money is in the other spouse's Canada Pension Plan or Quebec Pension Plan or Social Security Pension Plan? Is this balance to be divided or segregated and kept separate and intact?
12. Details of any medical/dental/prescription drug insurance provided through one spouse's employer? Is coverage to continue or stop? What about coverage for children of the marriage?

13. Regarding #12, what happens if the spouse or former spouse, whose employer provides group medical insurance, changes employment and the new employer does not provide similar or any coverage? What if the spouse/former spouse with the group medical coverage retires? Goes on disability?
14. Details of all joint credit cards? Who will pay off the outstanding balances? Is there a document reflecting a mutual agreement regarding payment?
15. A spousal interest in the business of the respondent, or the respondent a spousal interest in your business? Is there a document reflecting a mutual agreement regarding giving up the business interest, buying out the business interest, or whatever?

4 Checklist of Custody and Parental Visit Issues.

Use the Parenting Guide to help with this section

1. Who has custody in fact right now of the children of the marriage, if any?
2. Will custody arrangements stay the same after divorce?
3. What arrangements for child supervision will have to be made for a working parent with custody? Have arrangements been made already?
4. If the spouses are separated now, what visiting arrangements exist?
5. Are the visiting arrangements convenient for both parents?
6. Have the children been introduced to what is happening and will happen with the separation of the parents, the divorce proceedings, the custody arrangements and the parental visiting arrangements? Are they comfortable and satisfied with the arrangements?
7. Are the children prepared for and comfortable with discussing custody, visits, supervision, separation, divorce, and how they feel about these issues with an investigating child care caseworker or social worker? *{There is going to be one, you know. It's compulsory.)* Are they showing the same feelings and thoughts to the respondent spouse, or is the respondent hearing a different story?
8. Are you satisfied that the children have told you the truth about how they really feel about the arrangements that are being made for them, or are they just telling you what they think you want to hear? (In *my experience, children do that, you know, then surprise you at the most awkward time in public, when they feel the pressure is on. The solution is to prepare them well, do not deprive them of the stability and balance of exposure to both parents, unless absolutely necessary, and allow time for adjustment)*
9. Are there any past issues that the respondent spouse can use to damage your image as a proper and fit parent who deserves custody of the children? What are the specific key points against you?

____

____

10. How can you counter such accusations if you have to? What are the key points?

____

____

SEPARATION AGREEMENT

The separation agreement is needed even if your intention is to have a "friendly divorce" - one that both of you agree on.

The reason is that your charm, personality and good looks may buy you some goodwill in a handshake deal for now, but you can count on that to change later, once your former spouse has met someone else and has lost interest in you.

Also, how do you intend to prove that your memory is better than that of your ex-spouse's a year or two down the road when you two remember things differently.

When dealing with your life and perhaps the lives of your children, you should be as clear and precise in meaning as possible, to avoid mistakes and ambiguities - a clear, precise written document that represents the greatest certainty and best organization you can achieve.

Separation and divorce is an unpleasant business, it's better to deal with all the unpleasant things at one time. Get them over and out of the way as completely and comprehensively as possible so you don't have to revive these unpleasant feelings every time a new issue surfaces.

The agreement represents an all inclusive, comprehensive document that deals with a **messy situation** in a more organized way.

Some of the issues you will have to agree on are:

1. Living separately
2. Child custody
3. Visiting rights and schedule (see **parenting guide** for help)
4. Interim and permanent child support, if any
5. Interim and permanent spousal support, if necessary
6. Division of assets and liabilities
7. Provision for continuing health and life insurance, if any, and premium payment
8. Provision for a trust fund or insurance trust for children, if any
9. Provision for future dealing with proceeds of government pension plan benefits
   a.) Provision for dealing with employment pension benefits
   b.) Any other issues between the spouses.

Every jurisdiction has their own preferred style of agreements, including Separation Agreements. The following agreement outlines all the areas mentioned above. If you don't do your own agreement, at least you will be well informed so that you know your lawyer is doing a good job or you can do most of the preparatory work to minimize the lawyer's bill. An informed consumer is a happy one who won't fall victim.

With the possible exceptions of the Province of Quebec and the State of Louisiana, the form of

Separation agreement that follows is pretty much acceptable throughout North America. To get one of the forms used locally where you are, consult your local legal aid office. If it's different from the one that follows, you can modify it to your own needs.

What follows is a generic, general purpose form of separation agreement. You can delete the parts that do not apply to you.

SEPARATION AGREEMENT
&
PROPERTY SETTLEMENT

This Separation Agreement and Property Settlement made this_________ day of _________________, 2014

Between

____of the City of ______________________________

(Referred to in this agreement as the "husband")

And _______________________________________of the city of (referred to in this agreement as the "wife") and shall become effective as of the date that it has been executed by each party hereto.

WITNESSETH:
The parties were married to each other at _____________________________
In the Province/State Country ___________________________________ on

The _________________________day of ____________________, 2014

In the event that the marriage is dissolved the terms shall be construed to mean "former husband" and "former wife".

The husband and wife have ________ children, all of whom collectively called the "children" throughout and each of whom is individually called the "child" throughout.

Name of Child	Age	Date of Birth

As a result of irreconcilable differences between them, the husband and the wife have been living separate and apart since the__________ day of _____________, 2006 and each of them desires to settle by agreement all rights, claims, demands and causes of action which each has or may have against the other with respect to custody, maintenance, care and upbringing of the children, and with respect to their property, and with respect to any rights either or each of them has, or may have to alimony, maintenance or support from the other.

All the assets and liabilities of both the husband and wife are completely and accurately described in Schedule B, C and D attached to this agreement

This Agreement shall be a full and final settlement of their respective rights to and in property owned jointly and/or separately by them and

A full and final settlement of the issues of custody, access, guardianship and child support and

A full and final settlement of the issues of spousal support or maintenance.

WHEREAS each of the parties has made a full, complete disclosure of his/her financial circumstances including, but not limited to, all income, assets, bank/ trust accounts, RRSP's pensions, insurance policies and all debts and other liabilities and

WHEREAS each party has had an opportunity to seek independent legal counsel from the lawyer of his/her choice, each party believes it is in their best interests to enter into this separation agreement and property settlement and each party considers this agreement to be fair, reasonable and equitable and

WHEREAS each party wishes to voluntarily and entirely on their own free will enter into this agreement, and confirms that there are no outside pressures, compulsion or intimidation, and there is no power imbalance between the parties unduly influencing them to enter this agreement and

WHEREAS each party acknowledges and accepts that this agreement is not made in the hope of reconciliation or under the offer by the other of a possible reconciliation and that the separation is permenant.

THEREFORE, the husband and wife agree and acknowledge as follows:

LIVING SEPARATE AND APART – The husband and wife will continue living separate and apart from each other.

FREEDOM FROM THE OTHER - Neither husband or wife shall molest, annoy or in any way interfere with the other or use any means to compel, or attempt to compel, the other to Cohabit or live with him/her.

CUSTODY, ACCESS, GUARDIANSHIP - The husband and/or wife shall have sole/joint custody and the following children shall have their primary residence in the home of the husband/wife

Name of Child	Age	Date of Birth

The husband/wife shall have reasonable and generous access to the children on the terms outlined in Schedule A. neither the husband nor wife may permanently remove the children from ______________________________ without the consent in writing of the other.

The husband/wife will not interfere with, obstruct, block or otherwise prevent the scheduled access of the husband/wife to the children as outlined in Schedule A.

The husband/wife undertakes to notify the access parent of any problems, such as sickness of the children, which may prevent access, as much in advance as practical.Where an access visit is cancelled by the custodial parent, the access parent shall have an equal access makeup visit at a time of his/her choosing.

Both parties agree to refrain from all criticism and disparaging remarks about each other or any other disparaging or untoward behaviour in the presence of the children.The children shall not be used to carry messages or manipulated into choosing one parent over the other in any disagreement.

SEPARATION AGREEMENT
&
PROPERTY SETTLEMENT

This Separation Agreement and Property Settlement made this
_________ day of _________________, 2014

Between

____of the City of ________________________________

(Referred to in this agreement as the "husband")

And_______________________________________ of the city of (referred to in this agreement as the "wife")and shall become effective as of the date that it has been executed by each party hereto.

WITNESSETH:
The parties were married to each other at ______________________________
In the Province/State Country _____________________________________ on

The __________________________day of _____________________, 2014.

In the event that the marriage is dissolved the terms shall be construed to mean "former husband" and "former wife".

The husband and wife have ________ children, all of whom collectively called the "children" throughout and each of whom is individually called the "child" throughout.

Name of Child	Age	Date of Birth

As a result of irreconcilable differences between them, the husband and the wife have been living separate and apart since the __________________ day of _____________, 2014 and each of them desires to settle by agreement all rights, claims, demands and causes of action which each has or may have against the other with respect to custody, maintenance, care and upbringing of the children, and with respect to their property, and with respect to any rights either or each of them has, or may have to alimony, maintenance or support from the other.

All the assets and liabilities of both the husband and wife are completely and accurately described in **Schedules B, C and D** attached to this agreement.

This Agreement shall be a full and final settlement of their respective rights to and in property owned jointly and/or separately by them and

A full and final settlement of the issues of custody, access, guardianship and child support and A full and final settlement of the issues of spousal support or maintenance. **WHEREAS** each of the parties is more than 18 years of age and

WHEREAS each of the parties has a general knowledge of the other's financial and general circumstances and

WHEREAS each of the parties has made a full, complete disclosure of his/her financial circumstances including, but not limited to, all income, assets, bank/trust accounts, RRSP's, pensions, insurance policies and all debts and other liabilities and

WHEREAS each party has had an opportunity to seek independent legal counsel from the lawyer of his/her choice, each party believes it is in their best interests to enter into this separation agreement and property settlement and each party considers this agreement to be fair, reasonable and equitable and

WHEREAS each party has read this agreement, fully understands the terms, conditions and provisions hereof and deems such to be fair, just and equitable and

WHEREAS each party wishes to voluntarily and entirely on their own free will enter into this agreement, and confirms that there are no outside pressures, compulsion or intimidation, and there is no power imbalance between the parties unduly influencing them to enter this agreement and

WHEREAS each party acknowledges and accepts that this agreement is not made in the hope of reconciliation or under the offer by the other of a possible reconciliation and that the separation is permanent

THEREFORE, the husband and wife agree and acknowledge as follows:

LIVING SEPARATE AND APART - The husband and wife will continue living separate and apart from each other

FREEDOM FROM THE OTHER - Neither husband or wife shall molest, annoy or in any way interfere with the other or use any means to compel, or attempt to compel, the other to cohabit or live with him/her.

CUSTODY, ACCESS, GUARDIANSHIP - The husband and/or wife shall have sole/joint custody and the following children shall have their primary residence in the home of the husband/wife

Name of Child	Age	Date of Birth

The husband/wife shall have reasonable and generous access to the children on the terms outlined in **Schedule A.** neither the husband nor wife may permanently remove the children from ____________________ without the consent in writing of the other.

The husband/wife will not interfere with, obstruct, block or otherwise prevent the scheduled access of the husband/wife to the children as outlined in Schedule A.

The husband/wife undertakes to notify the access parent of any problems, such as sickness of the children, which may prevent access, as much in advance as practical. Where an access visit is cancelled by the custodial parent, the access parent shall have an equal access makeup visit at a time of his/her choosing.

Both parties agree to refrain from all criticism and disparaging remarks about each other or any other disparaging or untoward behavior in the presence of the children. The children shall not be used to carry messages or manipulated into choosing one parent over the other in any disagreement.

The custodial parent will facilitate access to all the children's school and medical records for the non custodial parent and will promptly provide written instructions or sign any necessary releases to school and medical authorities (when and as needed or requested) to release copies of all records and related information to the non custodial parent.

Both parents shall confer and share decisions on the children's education, medical care and the children's religious upbringing.

The parties agree that the children shall not be moved out of the court's jurisdictional or geographical area without written notice fourteen days in advance of any such move.

The parties agree that as long as access to the children is in effect, both parties will inform the other of their residential address and contact phones and notify the other party of any changes prior to their change and in no event more than two days after such change is made.

FINANCIALSUPPORT

Spousal support:

The husband/wife shall pay to the wife/husband, for his/her own support, the sum of

$__________ per month, commencing on the ___________ day of________________, 20__and continuing on each and every month thereafter until the ___________day of__________, 20____ or until such time as the husband/wife dies, remarries, or commences cohabitation with another person, in what is generally referred to as a common law relationship, or until the annual income of the wife/ husband from any and all other sources shall be $_________per annum, as evidenced by the Income Tax return of the husband/wife, or until the payer husband/wife dies, whichever comes first.

OR

The wife/husband waives all claims for support as the parties agree and acknowledge that each shall be self-supporting and is not in need of support from the other.

Child Support

The husband/wife shall pay to the wife/husband shall pay for the support of the children of the marriage until one of the following occurs:

i. the child becomes 16 years of age and ceases to be in full time attendance at an educational institution;
ii. the child ceases to reside with the custodial parent
iii. the child becomes 18 and is not enrolled in a recognized educational institution;

iv. the child obtains a post-secondary degree, diploma, completion certificate for a post secondary educational program, or the child becomes 21 years old, whichever occurs first;

v. the child resides more than 40% of the time with the non custodial parent;

vi. the child marries; or

vii. the child dies

Name of Child	Age	Date of Birth

$______________per month for each child for maintenance of that child based on guidelines

for the payer's annual income of $________________________.

Such payments shall be due and payable on the _______________ day of _______________, 20___and continuing on the ____________day of each month thereafter based on the above-noted conditions.

MATERIAL CHANGE IN CIRCUMSTANCES

i. The husband/wife intend for the financial support to be final except for variation by reason of material change in circumstances.

ii. Obligations arising out of the remarriage of the husband/wife are to be take into account in determining whether there is a material change in circumstances

iii. The husband/wife wanting the variation shall give the other a notice of the variation he/she is seeking and the husband/wife may then confer with each other personally or through their respective solicitors to settle what, if any variation should be made.

iv. If no agreement has been reached thirty clear days after notice has been given, a variation is to be determined upon application by either the husband or wife under the Family Law Act in force from time to time. (Note: Any legal references should be tailored to match the legal statutes in force in the applicable local jurisdiction)

HEALTH AND MEDICAL EXPENSES

i. The husband/wife warrants that he/she is maintaining in force for the benefit of the children, a health insurance plan (insert the name of the Medicare plan in force in the applicable local jurisdiction)

ii. The husband/wife agrees to continue this plan or an equivalent plan for the benefit of the children as long as required to provide support

iii. If the husband/wife fails to maintain this plan of insurance, he/she will become responsible for all medical/hospital expenses incurred by or on behalf of the custodial parent as long as he/she is required to provide support.

LIFE INSURANCE

i. The husband/wife shall immediately deliver to the custodial parent, true copies of all the existing policies of insurance on his/her life totaling $__________ in face value and consisting of: (insert policy numbers and insurance company names)

ii. The husband/ wife shall immediately designate the custodial parent as irrevocable beneficiary of these policies.

iii. The husband/wife agrees to maintain these policies of insurance in force for the benefit of the custodial parent and shall pay the premiums on each policy of insurance as each falls due until maturity of each policy

iv. If the custodial parent

a.) remarries, or

b.) lives with another person as if she had remarried, or

c.) dies

The husband/wife may substitute the child or children of the marriage as beneficiaries of the said policies and the wife/husband or his/her estate shall give any consent required to enable the husband/ wife to deal with these policies.

v. The husband/wife shall deliver a receipt to the custodial parent not later than 14 clear days following the date of payment of each premium under these policies and if the husband/wife defaults in payment of the premium the husband/wife may pay it and recover the amount with all costs and expenses in so doing including solicitor costs as between a solicitor and his own client.

ASSETTS AND LIABILITIES

Personal Property: The husband/wife each acknowledge that

i. all their personal property has been divided between them to their mutual satisfaction;

ii. each is entitled to the personal property now in his/her possession free from claim by the other; and

iii. each may dispose of the personal property now possessed by him/ her as if she/he were unmarried

MATRIMONIAL HOME

i. The husband/wife acknowledge that they hold as joint tenants the house and lot municipally known as ____ and each agrees that it will continue to be held jointly by both parties subject to the terms of "Schedule B"

PENSION PLAN

Both parties agree that any credits and benefits accruing to either party will be shared in accordance with equal division rules as established by government regulations

OTHER ASSETTS

All other assets are listed and shared in accordance with **Schedule C**

DEBTS AND OBLIGATIONS

(i) Neither the husband nor the wife shall contract in the name of the other nor in any way bind the other for any debts or obligations

(ii) If debts or obligations are incurred by the husband/wife on behalf of the other before or after the date of this agreement, he or she shall indemnify the other

from all claims, costs, expenses, damages and actions arising from those debts or obligations.

RELEASE

(i) The husband and the wife each accept the terms of this agreement in satisfaction of all claims and causes of action each now has except for claims and causes of action arising out of this agreement or for a decree of divorce; including but not limited to claims and causes of action for custody, child maintenance, spousal support, maintenance, interim support, possession of or title to property, and any other claims arising out of marriage of the husband/wife.

(ii) Nothing in this agreement constitutes a bar to any action or proceeding of either the husband or wife to enforce any of the terms of this agreement.

SEPARATION AGREEMENT TO SURVIVE DIVORCE

If either the husband or the wife obtains a decree of divorce, all the terms of this agreement shall survive and continue in force. If either the husband or the wife obtains a decree of divorce, the terms "former husband" and "former wife" shall be substituted for the terms husband and wife used in this agreement.

EXECUTION OF OTHER DOCUMENTS

The husband and wife shall at any time and from time to time execute and deliver to the other any document or documents that the other reasonably requires to give effect to the terms of this agreement.

INVALIDITY

In the event that any clause contained herein is found by a court of competent jurisdiction to be invalid and unenforceable, this agreement shall be henceforth read and interpreted as if that clause were never a part of this agreement and the remaining clauses of this agreement shall henceforth be read and interpreted as much as they can be, mutais mutandis, *as a consistent whole, without the deleted clause or clauses, (mutais mutandis=with such changes as necessary)

JURISDICTION

Jurisdiction shall lie initially with the court of competent jurisdiction in the judicial jurisdiction in which the husband and wife reside together as husband and wife. If they no longer reside in the same jurisdiction then any party having legal standing may apply to any court having competent jurisdiction. If an issue of conflict of jurisdiction or of lack of jurisdiction is raised

and cannot be agreed on by the parties on consent, such issue or issues, which court or authority having competence to resolve such issue or issues, which court or authority may then refer by order such matters as it finds appropriate to such *"forum conveniens* " as it deems appropriate for resolution. *(forum conveniens=most* convenient court)

DISPUTE RESOLUTION

The parties prefer to settle any differences, which may arise under this agreement between themselves without recourse to the courts except after exhausting all other reasonable means of dispute resolution. Accordingly, the parties agree to follow these procedures for dispute resolution before making any applications to the court.

The party wishing to resolve the dispute will provide written notice of his/her intention to invoke the Dispute Resolution section of this agreement.

Both parties will attempt to resolve any disputes either directly between themselves or with the assistance of their lawyers.

If the dispute is not settled after 14 consecutive days have elapsed since giving written notice, either party may refer the matter for resolution by mediation at joint expense

The mediator shall be an individual agreed on by both parties. Failing agreement, each party shall choose a mediator and those mediators shall choose a third mediator or the parties may nominate a mutually agreeable person to choose a mediator from a suitable list of candidates proposed by the parties or their lawyers.

Should mediation fail and the parties remain unable to resolve their differences either party may on 14 days notice to the other take appropriate proceedings in court. Costs of these proceedings shall be determined and allocated between the parties by the court.

Both parties agree to cooperate fully with the mediation process and attend all reasonable appointments made by the mediator.

Execution

65. TO EVIDENCE THEIR AGREEMENT, the parties have each signed this agreement SIGNED SEALED AND DELIVERED

Print name ______________________________	Print Name ______________________________
Sign name ______________________________	Sign name ______________________________
(Witness)	***(Spouse)***
Print name ______________________________	Print Name ______________________________
Sign name ______________________________	Sign name ______________________________
(Witness)	***(Spouse)***

DATED______________________________, 20_____ _____

CERTIFICATE AND AFFIDAVIT OF WITNESS

I,___________________________________of the city of_________________________________in the Province/Territory of____________________

MAKE OATH or AFFIRM AND SAY

1. I am a witness to this Separation Agreement between ______________________________ and ___________________________ and saw __________________________________execute it at the City of __________________________________
2. I verily believe that the person whose signature I witnessed is the party of the same named referred to in the Separation Agreement.
3. I believe that __________________________________is fully aware of the nature and effect of this Separation Agreement and is signing the document voluntarily.
4. I know that the person whose signature I witnessed is fully able to read and understand this agreement.

Sworn or Affirmed before me at

the city of______________________

in the Municipality of _____________

this __________ day of _________ 20___

Print name ___________________________

Sign name ___________________________

____

Commissioner for taking affidavits

Affidavit of Witness to sep agreement.wpd

Schedule A

Time Table for Access to the Child(ren)

(If necessary, prepare schedules for each child)

Be very specific about times, dates, pick up and drop off locations and any notice required for changes to any given visit.

Period	**Specify precise dates, times, locations of pickup & drop off**
Weekends	
Mid Week	
Telephone access	
Christmas Holidays	
March School Break	
Summer vacation	
Access to School reports	
Access to Medical reports	

Describe how missed access visits are to be made up:

Describe how changes to this schedule will be made:

Both parties should initial this schedule ____________________ ____________________

Schedule A Access timetable. wpd

Schedule B

Matrimonial Home

The matrimonial home is situated at

____

____

It currently has a fair market value of approximately $ ___________________

and carries mortgages in the amount of approximately $ _________________

The Husband/Wife shall have exclusive possession and occupation of the matrimonial home which is at ____ rent free, until such time as the parties mutually agree to sell the home. During said occupancy the husband/wife will maintain the premises properly, pay all mortgage payments, taxes, insurance, and all utilities promptly and on time.

If the parties cannot agree on when the home should be sold, or on the terms and conditions of such a sale, either may apply to the Court for an order resolving these issues. When the home is sold, the net equity or loss resulting from the sale, (sale price minus real estate commission, mortgage(s), taxes, legal costs and other related expenses) shall be divided equally between the parties.

OR

Immediately upon execution of this agreement, the Husband/Wife shall purchase from the Husband/ Wife all interests, rights and title to and in the matrimonial home upon the following terms and conditions:

The payment to the Husband/Wife of the sum of$____

(List other terms and conditions) ____
_

____
_

OR

On or about the ________ day of___________________, 20__, the matrimonial home was

sold and proceeds were divided to the complete satisfaction of the Husband and Wife and each hereby agrees not claim or bring any claim or action regarding the matrimonial home against the other for any reasons whatsoever.

Both parties should initial this schedule ________________________ ________________________

Strike out and initial any clauses which do not apply.

Schedule B Matrimonial Home.wpd

Schedule C

Disposition of All Family Assets

The **husband** shall have and hereafter exclusively own and possess the following assets. The wife forever renounces any equity, ownership, rights to, claim or colour of right to these items.

Description	**Estimated Replacement Value**
Household Items	
Vehicles	
RRSPs, Investments, Savings bonds etc	
Other	

Both parties should initial this schedule______________________ ______________________

Schedule C Assets disposition.wpd

Schedule C

Disposition of All Family Assets

The **wife** shall have and hereafter exclusively own and possess the following assets. The wife forever renounces any equity, ownership, rights to, claim or colour of right to these items.

Description	**Estimated Replacement Value**
Household Items	
Vehicles	
RRSPs, Investments, Savings bonds etc	
Other	

Both parties should initial this schedule ________________________ ________________________

Schedule C Assets disposition.wpd

Schedule D

Disposition of All Family Liabilities

The Husband shall forthwith accept all liability and releases the Wife from all obligations for the following

Institution Holding Account	Account #	Current balance	Payments

The Wife shall forthwith accept all liability and releases the Husband from all obligations for the following

Institution Holding Account	Account #	Current balance	Payments

Both parties should initial this schedule ______________________ ______________________

Schedule D Liabilities disposition.wpd and

____

and

____

SEPARATION AND PROPERTY AGREEMENT

ii) Claim/Petition For Divorce

There are too many different jurisdictions in North America and there are too many different forms of Claim or Petition for Divorce to be collected and included here. Obtain a blank copy in your jurisdiction from your local legal forms printing company, from a cooperative lawyer, from a local legal aid clinic, or from your own source.

You should have no problem completing the preliminary part of the form, if you have read the check lists in Chapter 2 and you are ready according to them.

Note also how the heading on the first page is laid out. This is where the court, the jurisdiction, the names of the parties to the divorce proceeding and the title of the document are set out. This is called the "Style of Cause" and is repeated on every document you prepare for the court. Be certain to pay attention to this detail and get it right. Court staff can be very particular about such details of form. If you get it wrong, your documents may be thrown back to you with a demand that you do them again.

After the section dealing with the preliminary vital statistics of the parties, the next section will concentrate on those "substantive" (as lawyers call them) issues such as the grounds, particulars of the grounds and corollary (additional) relief sought. The wrong choice of words can trip you up and deny you what you want when you finally get before the divorce court. Choose your words carefully, both on paper and in live testimony. Double check what you say and how you say it with a person of some experience or a professional. The court and the judge will not be very forgiving of errors and will be impatient with disorganization, hesitation, lack of preparation, or unfamiliarity with procedure and the basic requirements. Ask lots of questions of those who know. You can do this if you prepare and practice. But you will have only one chance to get it right.

We shall consider firstly the statement of the grounds for divorce, ground by ground. If you do not state the grounds correctly, you will not get your divorce judgment. You will stand there, papers in hand, probably with your mouth hanging open, speechless, with no divorce judgment, and with the court clerk briskly calling the next case. You will be a Loser. Everyone there will snicker at you. That's the penalty for doing it wrong.

We shall next consider the statement of the relief sought, in various alternative forms. Again, if you do not ask, specifically and clearly, for each and every item of relief that you actually want, the judge will be powerless to give it to you, because to do so without notice would be prejudicial to the respondent spouse. You will have had your day in court and now face yet another court procedure to fix what you got wrong the first time. Talk about being a Loser!

In the following pages are the tools to make your efforts pay off as well or better than any professional lawyer would do. Unfortunately, it is not possible to foresee every possible situation in the world, so you must keep your wits about you and make sure you yourself cover all the points you need. Take responsibility yourself. Don't just rely on these words. But do look for the patterns in the examples that follow and then add on, subtract from, or embellish them as you see fit. Double check your own work by having the cleverest, most experienced person you know proofread your draft. The local court clerk in your local court filing office may also be able to point out certain ambiguities, oddities, or omissions in your choices of wordings, thus helping you to improve your final version. They will not go too far or be too specific giving you help, though, because that would be giving you legal advice. They are not supposed to do so.

One final very important point. Obtain a copy of the actual divorce legislation applicable in your jurisdiction. Get the actual Divorce Act, not some book, article or pamphlet that explains it or talks about it. Read the section on Grounds for Divorce. It should be fairly close to the beginning. You sill understand enough of what you read to be able to find where it states the ground for divorce that you wish to rely on. Now, when you are drafting your statement of your own ground for divorce in your own divorce application, try to stay as close as possible to the wording in the Divorce Act. That is what you actually have to prove to the divorce court.

Where the Grounds are Marriage Breakdown

1 Single Petitione

There has been a permanent breakdown of the marriage by reason of the fact that the Petitioner (Applicant) and the Respondent have lived separate and apart for at least one year prior to the commencement of this proceeding.

2 Joint Petition

There has been a permanent breakdown of the marriage by reason of the fact that the Petitioner (Applicant) and Respondent have agreed to live separate and apart and have on their mutual agreement lived separate and apart for at least one year prior to the commencement of this proceeding.

3 Where the Grounds are Adultery

The Respondent, while married to the Petitioner (Applicant) and not separated or living apart form the Petitioner (Applicant), has committed an act or acts of adultery with the Co-Respondent, which has or have not been forgiven or condoned.

4 Where the Grounds are Physical Cruelty

The Respondent, while married to the Petitioner (Applicant), physically assaulted the Petitioner (Applicant) *(alternative, if applicable:* repeatedly committed acts of assault on the person of the Petitioner (Applicant)) and caused significant bodily harm which required medical attention.

5 Where the Grounds are Mental Cruelty

The Respondent, while married to the Petitioner (Applicant), committed acts of such cruelty towards the Petitioner (Applicant) as to require psychiatric (or psychological) care and treatment and of such a significant degree as to render intolerable the continuation of the marriage.

6 Alcoholism or Substance Abuse - a possible treatment

Through uncontrolled alcoholism/narcotic substance abuse the Respondent has created such a significantly unhealthy and unfit environment as to constitute significant regular and continued mental cruelty to a degree that the Petitioner (Applicant) required psychological counseling and treatment and to such a degree as to render the continuation of the marriage intolerable.

(CAUTION: You had better seek legal advice before attempting to use the last one. I am including it merely to

show how alcoholism and drug abuse could possibly befit into the existing framework of present statutory legal authority. There is no claim as to its legal validity as a divorce ground at the time this is written.)

(iii) Affidavit of Service

After you have filed your application/or divorce in the court clerk's office you must serve exact copies, called true copies, personally on every person you have named as a respondent. Once you have done so you must complete the following statement, signed and sworn before a lawyer or official authorized to take oaths, stating the fact that you have delivered a true copy to the appropriate person. This sworn statement, called an Affidavit, must be attached to the original divorce application and filed in the court clerk's office after the mandatory waiting period for a response has elapsed and before you are permitted to set your divorce case on the trial waiting list.

For procedural reasons having to do with court procedure it is better to have service of the documents per formed by an outside, independent person rather than by you yourself. There are plenty of professional process servers and paralegals in any local phone book who can perform this little task correctly and efficiently, and who will even prepare the signed and sworn Affidavit of Service for you for a modest charge. This is the recommended approach, not only for the sake of getting it right, but to avoid any unpleasant incidents or confrontations at a very sensitive stage of the proceedings. But if you insist on doing this yourself, or having a friend do this, then see a suitable sample form of Affidavit of Service below.

If the whereabouts of the Respondent are not known, you must make a special motion to a judge, consisting of a written application and a supporting affidavit, requesting that service be dispensed with or alternatively substituted service by advertisement of the divorce application in the legal column of a widely disseminated newspaper. At this point you should consider professional legal assistance.

AFFIDAVIT OF SERVICE

Style of Cause

(i.e. Case Heading)

I, ______*(state your name)*________, of the City/Town of________________________, in the County/Judicial District of______________, in the Province/State of ________________, do solemnly make oath and say:

1) I have personal knowledge of the facts deposed to herein.

2) I served the Respondent in this proceeding, Mr./Mrs. ______________________, with a true copy of the _____*name the document*________attached hereto by delivering the same to him/her at _ ________*state time of day*______more or less, at:

Insert exact address & zip/postal code

(Insert the applicable clauses from the examples below or insert your own.)

3) I asked the Respondent to identify him/herself and he/she admitted to me that he/she is ______*insert Respondent's name*______, the Respondent named in this proceeding.

4) I asked the Respondent to produce further identification and he/she complied by producing valid_________*state or province*_________ drivers license no.______________________.

5) Attached is a photograph of the Respondent taken by me when I performed service ***(OR*** Attached is a photograph of the Respondent provided by him/her to me when I performed service. I have compared the appearance of the person in the photo with the person I served and they appear to me to be one and the same person.

6) This Affidavit is made in support of this divorce proceeding as proof of service of the attached document and for no improper purpose.

SWORN BEFORE ME at the

City of ___________, in the County/Judicial

District of _________, this_______day ________________

of______________, 2_____.

Commissioner of oaths or Notary Public **(iv)**

Affidavits Supporting the Petitioner's Allegations

In an uncontested divorce, where the Respondent does not file a dispute, the Applicant submits the supporting evidence in the form. of an Affidavit (sworn statement) and notes the court file closed without any filings by the Respondent. The rather uncomplimentary name for this step in the procedure, performed after the compulsory waiting period after service has elapsed, is "Noting the Respondent in Default, Closing Pleadings, Passing the Record and Setting Down the Proceeding on the Trial List".

Sometimes, in some jurisdictions, if there is no dispute filed by the Respondent, the procedure is to do a Motion for Default Judgment. Then the Affidavit in Support is titled Affidavit in Support of Motion for Default Judgment.

In general, these Affidavits In Support are sworn statements of all the facts and details you want to put before the divorce judge for him to consider while deciding on your divorce application.

State all the facts clearly, simply and in chronological order. Do not omit any relevant facts or details but do not drone on with unnecessary side issues or your life story. That can only serve to confuse and bore the judge.

Many times, when I was a young practitioner before the courts I experienced a judge who would focus in on what I considered a minor, casually mentioned small point, mentioned for colour or emphasis. The judge would find in some minor point an objectionable issue and draw me onto a tangent where I did not want to be. The solution to this problem of being side-tracked is to plan in advance what to say, make an outline, rehearse, and then stick scrupulously to your outline. Answer any judge's question clearly, concisely, to the point, and then redirect the conversation back to your main presentation and carry on where you left off.

Remember your main points and concentrate on them, one at a time, as n your outline. Be sure to state facts that tend to prove convincingly that you have good grounds for your divorce. You are required to state enough so as not to mislead the court as to the true nature of the situation, but you are under no obligation to state absolutely every fact you know. State nothing that you cannot prove with an eyewitness or documentary backup as proof. State nothing that is not in direct proof of one of your main points. Do not try to state and argue points that are weak or only loosely related to your main points. If a judge shows he rejects or disagrees with the implication you are trying to make from some fact, do not argue with the judge, just move on to the next point and try to make your case another way.

You must state every main point of fact that you wish to rely on when you appear before the judge, so be thorough. But at the same time be brief. The judge is interested in your history, but not your histrionics. Keep your Affidavit in Support to a maximum of 3 pages. As long as you state all the necessary main points, you can supplement them with supporting details if necessary at the hearing.

In some jurisdictions an unopposed divorce application is reviewed without a live hearing before a divorce judge at all. In these jurisdictions, the application and all supporting evidence are in writing, handed in at the clerk's office, and reviewed privately by a judge whom you never do get to meet or appear before. It is even more crucial in this case to state just enough detail to convince the unseen judge that you have satisfied the legal requirement and that you should get what you ask for. Be easily understood. Use short sentences. Be thorough. But be brief.

(iv - i) **Marriage Breakdown - Single Petitioner**

[Style of Cause]

a) I have personal knowledge of the facts deposed to herein.

b) The Respondent and I separated on or about____*date*____and since then have continuously maintained entirely separate residences and lives, and continue to do so to this date.

c) The child (children) of the marriage have all resided with me since the separation. They are in regular attendance at educational institutions and they are making satisfactory progress. Particulars are as follows:

NAME	BIRTH DATE	SCHOOL	GRADE

d) I do not work and I can provide all necessary home supervision. *(OR:* I am employed but I have arranged for responsible home supervision for the children of the marriage with name *the child_sitter* and there has been no problem with this arrangement nor any objection by the Respondent to this arrangement. The Respondent has not made any other custody or child care arrangements.

e) Child visiting arrangements have been discussed and settled and appear to be working well and satisfactory between the parties. Particulars of the child visit arrangements are:(Set out the arrangements in detail here. It is OK to copy from your Separation Agreement if it has been signed.)

f) The Respondent has not requested any change to these arrangements or made provision for any other visiting arrangements.

g) Support arrangements for me and for the child/children of the marriage have been discussed and settled and are satisfactory to both the parties. Particulars of the support arrangements are: *(Set out* the arrangements in detail here. It is OK to copy from your Separation Agreement, if it has been signed.)

h) Property, insurance and other matters between the parties have been discusses and settled and are satisfactory to both parties. Particulars of he matters discussed and arranged are: *(Set* out any other arrangements in detail here. It is OK to copy from your Separation Agreement, if it has been signed.)

i) The parties have executed a Separation Agreement, dated *date* , in which they have agreed to all matters regarding:

i.	Child custody	clause
ii.	Child visits	clause
iii.	Spousal support	clause
iv.	Child support	clause
v.	Property division	clause
vi.	Life insurance	clause
vii.	Health insurance	clause
viii.	Pensions	clause

ix. (add anything else that needs mentioning)

j) There is no attempt in progress or contemplated to revise the provisions of the said Separation Agreement. I respectfully request the court to consider and include the foregoing listed provisions in a judgment for divorce, along with any other provisions that it deems appropriate.

k) It would clearly not be appropriate in the circumstances for the court to consider the possibility of the reconciliation of the spouses because:

{Choose an applicable example or insert your own.)

i. the spouses have already exhaustively attempted reconciliation talks and have sought professional marriage counseling, but all attempts have failed and neither of the spouses are willing to make any further effort to reconcile;

ii. the Applicant/Respondent spouse has already formed an exclusive relationship with another person in which they live as man and wifeCO-R and they intend to marry as soon as they are free to do so/ in the future);

iii. The Respondent has moved away to another city/to the City of ________ and has demonstrated thereby that there is no desire to have any further ongoing relationship;

iv. Because of the facts surrounding the cruelty of the Respondent towards the Applicant, it would be intolerable for the Applicant to reconcile with the Respondent and continue the spousal relationship and it would be a clear danger to the health of the Applicant to do so.

l) (IF THERE IS A REQUEST FOR AN IMMEDIATE JUDGMENT ABSOLUTE OF DIVORCE, RATHER THAN THE USUAL INTERIM JUDGMENT AND WAITING PERIOD) I respectfully request that this court grant an immediate absolute and final judgment of divorce for the following urgent

Example:

I have formed a new exclusive relationship with a person I intend to marry. We are expecting the imminent birth of our child and we wish to be married before the child is born, for the sake of the legitimacy of the child. I hereby irrevocably undertake not to appeal a divorce absolute granted by this court in the terms I seek. A similar undertaking not to appeal a divorce absolute granted by this court in the terms I seek signed by the Respondent is attached hereto.

m) This Affidavit is made in support of the divorce proceeding between the parties and for no purpose of delay or improper purpose.

SWORN BEFORE ME at the

City of ______________, in the County/Judicial

District of _____________,this______day _______________

of______,2__.__

Commissioner of oaths
or Notary Public

(iv-ii) Marriage Breakdown- Joint Petition

(Joint Divorce Petitions are available in Canada, but not in all of North America.)

[Style of Cause]

1. We, the Applicant and Respondent in this proceeding, have personal knowledge of the facts deposed to herein.

2. We, the Applicant and Respondent, separated on or about *date* by mutual agreement. Since then we have continuously maintained entirely separate residences and lives and we continue to do so to this date.

3. The child (children) of the marriage have all resided with the Applicant since the separation. They are in regular attendance at educational institutions and they are making satisfactory progress. Particulars are as follows:

NAME	BIRTH DATE	SCHOOL	GRADE

4. I, the Applicant, do not work and I can provide all necessary home supervision. *(OR:* I, the Applicant, am employed but I have arranged for responsible home supervision for the children of the marriage with *name the child sitter* during my working hours and there has been no problem with this arrangement nor any objection by the Respondent to this arrangement. The Respondent has not made any other custody or child care arrangements.

5. Child visiting arrangements have been discussed and settled by mutual agreement and appear to be satisfactory and working well between the parties. Particulars of the child visit arrangements are:

(Set out the arrangements in detail here. It is OK to copy from your Separation Agreement if it has been signed.)

6. The Respondent has not requested any change to these arrangements, arrived at my mutual consent, nor made provision for any other visiting arrangements.

7. Support arrangements for me and for the child/children of the marriage have been discussed and settled by mutual agreement and are satisfactory to both the parties. Particulars of the support arrangements are:

(Set out the arrangements in detail here. It is OK to copy from your Separation Agreement, if it has been signed.)

8. Property, insurance and other matters between the parties have been discusses and settled by mutual agreement and are satisfactory to both parties. Particulars of he matters discussed and arranged are:

(Set out any other arrangements in detail here. It is OK to copy from your Separation Agreement, if it has been signed.)

9. The parties have executed a Separation Agreement, dated *date* . in which they have mutually agreed to all matters regarding:

a.	Child custody	clause	e. Property division	clause
b.	Child visits	clause	f. Life insurance	clause
c.	Spousal support	clause	g. Health insurance	clause

d. Child support clause h. Pensions clause

i. *(add anything else that needs mentioning)*

10. There is no attempt in progress or contemplated to revise the provisions of the said Separation Agreement. We respectfully request the court to consider and include the foregoing listed provisions in a judgment for divorce, along with any other provisions that it deems appropriate.

11. It would clearly not be appropriate in the circumstances for the court to consider the possibility of the reconciliation of the spouses because the spouses have already exhaustively attempted reconciliation talks and have sought professional marriage counseling, but all attempts have failed and neither of the spouses are willing to make any further effort to reconcile.

12. (IF *THERE IS A REQUEST FOR AN IMMEDIATE JUDGMENT ABSOLUTE OF DIVORCE, RATHER THAN THE USUAL INTERIM JUDGMENT AND WAITING PERIOD)* We respectfully request that this court grant an immediate absolute and final judgment of divorce for the following urgent reason:

Examples:

a. I, the Applicant/Respondent, have formed a new exclusive relationship with a person I intend to marry. We are expecting the imminent birth of our child and we wish to be married before the child is born, for the sake of the legitimacy of the child.

b. We, the Applicant and Respondent, as spouses, have already exhaustively attempted reconciliation talks and *(if applicable)* have sought professional marriage counseling, but all attempts have failed and neither of the spouses are willing to make any further effort to reconcile.

13. I, the Applicant, hereby irrevocably undertake not to appeal a divorce absolute granted by this court in the terms we seek.

14. I, the Respondent, also irrevocably undertake not to appeal a divorce absolute granted by this court in the terms we seek

15. This Affidavit is made in support of the divorce proceeding between the parties and for no purpose of delay or improper purpose.

SWORN BEFORE ME at the City of ___________,

in the County/Judicial district of _____________,

this______day of______, 2__.__

Commissioner of oaths

or NotaryPublic .(iv-iii) Adultery

(Adultery requires 2 independent sources of proof for judicial acceptance.)

[Style of Cause]

1. I, the Applicant in this proceeding, have personal knowledge of the facts deposed to herein.

2. *(Specific acts) of adultery)* The Respondent and the Co-Respondent committed an act of adultery on or about the________ day of_________, 2____, at_____________ *address* at about

the hour of ___*time* . *(OR)* The Respondent and Co-Respondent committed repeated and regular acts of adultery together most Wednesday and Friday evenings (or weekends) over the period beginning about *date* and ending about _*date* *(or)* and continuing to the present time at the Co-Respondent's residence at _________*address*_________________ and/or at the Alpha Hotel, the Beta Hotel, the Gamma Hotel, and various other locations about the city.

3. *(Non-specific acts of adultery)* Particulars of the alleged adultery (adulteries) complained of are as follows:

The Respondent and Co-Respondent are keeping regular company with each other, openly and publicly, and are conducting themselves and are generally regarded by their friends and by strangers interacting with them alike as a romantic couple. They frequently dine together in public restaurants and at the Co-Respondent's home, attend movies and the theatre together, attend parties and social gatherings together, have been on trips together, and frequently stay overnight at each other's home. They have never taken the trouble to deny their romantic relationship and seem to tacitly acknowledge that once this divorce proceeding is over they will intensify their relationship into a common law relationship, sharing the same residence as man and wife, or even legally marry.

4. My means of knowledge of these occurrences are as follows: *(Choose an applicable form or compose your own)*

i. The Respondent admitted the act(s) of adultery to me as described above.

ii. The Respondent and Co-Respondent have been living together openly as man and wife since or about *date* at ________address________ and continue to do so to this date.

iii. The Respondent and Co-Respondent were seen by Mr./Ms. _______, a private investigator,__ to enter theCo-Respondent's residence at _________*address* and to remain there together until the following morning. A true copy of that written report is attached hereto as Exhibit "A".

iv. The Respondent and Co-Respondent were seen by Mr./Ms.____________________, a private investigator,_to enter the Co-Respondent's residence at *address* and to remain there together until the following morning. A true copy of that written report is attached hereto as Exhibit "A".

v. The Respondent and Co-Respondent were seen by Mr./Ms. _______________, the next door neighbour, who resides at _____*address* , to enter the Co-Respondent's residence at ______*address* and to remain there together until the following morning. A true copy of that written report is attached hereto as Exhibit "A"

vi. The Respondent and Co-Respondent were seen by Mr./Ms.______________, to enter the lobby of the Alpha Hotel, ________address________, where he/she works as a registration clerk, on or about *date* where they registered for a room and then retired to it. A true copy of an Affidavit to this effect signed by Mr./Ms.___________________ is attached hereto as Exhibit "B".

vii. The Respondent and Co-Respondent were seen by Mr./Ms. _______________, to enter the lobby of the Beta Hotel, ________address________where he/she works as a registration clerk, at various times between __date___ and_*date* , where they would routinely register for a room and then retire to it. A true copy of an Affidavit to this effect signed by Mr./Ms. _______________ is attached hereto as

Exhibit "B", and attached to his/her Affidavit is a true copy of extracts from the guest registry of the Beta Hotel showing the dates and times of registration by the Respondent and Co-Respondent.

5. I have neither forgiven nor condoned the Respondent's act(s) of adultery to this day, nor will I.

6. It would clearly not be appropriate in the circumstances for the court to consider the possibility of the reconciliation of the spouses because the spouses have already exhaustively attempted reconciliation talks and *(.if applicable)* have sought professional marriage counseling, but all attempts have failed and neither of the spouses are willing to make any further effort to reconcile;

7. This Affidavit is made in support of the allegations of adultery in this proceeding and for no improper purpose or delay.

SWORN BEFORE ME at the City of ______________,

in the County/Judicial district of ________________,

this _____ day of __________, 2_____. _____

Commissioner of oaths or Notary Public

iv-iv-i Physical Cruelty

(Physical cruelty usually requires 2 independent sources of proof, one of them being a medical or police source or record.)

[Style of Cause]

1. I, the Applicant in this proceeding, have personal knowledge of the facts deposed to herein.

2. The Respondent committed an act of physical cruelty against me on or about the_day of ______, 2____, at________address________at about the hour of ____*time*____by *(Name the specific act of cruelty).*

3. The Respondent committed repeated and regular acts of physical cruelty against me most weekends over the period beginning about _*date* and ending about_*date* *(or)* and continuing to the present time at our matrimonial residence at________address________ and/or at the Belly Buster Burger Bar, _ *address,* on or about_*date* , and at the wedding reception of my niece, on or about _ *date.* Particulars of the Respondent's acts of physical cruelty are as follows:

i. Most weekends during the period between_____*date*_____ and _*date* the Respondent would get drunk, consuming about 20 to 30 bottles of beer a day and a 26 ounce bottle of rye. He would then make demands that I instantly have food ready for him, and when I would ask him what he wanted he would shove me roughly, push me into the wall, knocking me onto the floor, grab my arm and yank me up slap and punch me about the face, head and upper body and cause me to flee for my safety to a neighbour's house. Attached as Exhibits "A" through "E" are 3 police incident reports and 2 Emergency Department medical reports. Exhibit "E" reflects the same incident as Exhibit "F", which is a true copy of a medical report from my personal doctor, indicating that on the last occasion I sustained 2 cracked ribs and a broken finger as a result of the most recent physical assault of the Respondent.

ii. On the occasion mentioned at the Belly Buster Burger Bar, on or about _*date* the Respondent consumed half a hamburger and 4 beers and then suddenly became enraged at me for no apparent reason that I can determine. He flung his plate of unfinished hamburger and fries at my face, tossed a glass of water in my face, soaking my blouse, and shouted "You're a freaking cow!" for all to hear. I felt embarrassed and humiliated and ran crying into the ladies washroom and I would not come out until a half hour later when a sympathetic waitress came in and told me that the Respondent had left without me. There was no call for police on that occasion and therefore no police incident report, but I did return to find the waitress that I mentioned. Her Affidavit stating what happened is attached as Exhibit "G".

iii. At my niece's wedding reception, on or about_*date* , there was an open bar. The Respondent consumed at least 8 bottles of beer and numerous shots of liquor, probably mostly rye. When we were dancing the Respondent could not keep his balance, nearly falling, and was clumsy moving his feet. He became enraged, slapped my face and called me a clumsy cow loudly enough for the whole room of my relatives, the groom's family and guests to hear. I was mortified in front of all my family and new nephew's family and I ran outside and sat in our car. About ten minutes later the Respondent followed me into our car, proceeded to berate me for leaving him, and slapped and punched me further, hard, about my face. I cried and begged him to stop until he did and drove us home. I then spent the rest of the night hiding in our second bedroom while the Respondent slept off his drink in the master bedroom. I had a bruise just under my left eye and a cut lower lip for the next two weeks. I did not report the incident to the police or seek medical help as I was not that seriously hurt on that occasion. My said niece and nephew have completed an Affidavit confirming the facts, which is attached hereto as Exhibit "H".

iv. I have tried to discuss the Respondent's drinking problem with him. He denies that there is any problem and just gets angry when I try to discuss it again. I am afraid to arouse his anger, so I have stopped trying to discuss it.

v. I believe that the Respondent's heavy drinking is likely to continue and I have no reason to believe that his drinking will stop. I have every reason to believe that as his drinking becomes heavier and more frequent so will his violent behaviour towards me. I am in fear for my safety and I believe that if we continue together there is a real and imminent possibility that he may seriously.

5. It would clearly not be appropriate in the circumstances for the court to consider the possibility of the reconciliation of the spouses because of the facts surrounding the cruelty of the Respondent towards the Applicant. It would be intolerable for the Applicant to reconcile with the Respondent and continue the spousal relationship and it would be a clear danger to the health of the Applicant to do so. The Applicant has neither forgiven nor condoned the behaviour of the Respondent, nor is the Applicant willing to do so.

6. This Affidavit is made in support of the allegations of adultery in this proceeding and for no improper purpose or delay.

SWORN BEFORE ME at the City of ______________,

in the County/Judicial district of ________________,

this _____ day of __________, 2__.__

Commissioner of oaths or Notary Public

Public .iv-iv-ii Mental Cruelty

(Mental cruelty usually requires 2 independent sources of proof, one of them being a psychiatric source.)

[Style of Cause]

1. I, the Applicant in this proceeding, have personal knowledge of the facts deposed to herein.

2. The Respondent committed a series of acts amounting to mental cruelty towards me over the past ______ months and continues to do so up to the present time by *(Name the specific act of cruelty.)*

Example:

Nearly every evening for the past two years and nearly every weekend the Respondent berates me, belittles me and launches into a long monologue of sarcastic comments criticizing nearly everything I do. According to the Respondent I don't dress right, I don't conduct myself right, I don't speak intelligently, I don't keep house right, I don't cook right, I don't drive right, I don't understand events or people right, I am stupid, ugly, sloppy, incapable and boring. I have been completely unable to please or satisfy the Respondent over the past two years. I have become such a nervous wreck that am constantly depressed, frequently cry for no apparent reason, have frequent thoughts of suicide and feel utterly alone and unable to carry on with my job and my daily life. At the urging of family and friends I have sought medical help and I am now in the care of a psychiatrist, Dr. R. U. Betterer. I am taking the prescription drug __________, which is a mood enhancer and mood stabilizer. I am certain that if I were to continue in the present relationship with the Respondent I would quickly and inevitably become completely incapacitated and unable to cope with my job and with my daily life. Continuing in a relationship with the Respondent is intolerable to me and I am certain it would utterly destroy me emotionally.

3. The Respondent committed repeated and regular acts amounting to mental cruelty towards me most weekends over the period beginning about__*date* and ending about __*date* (or) and continuing to the present time at our matrimonial residence at _______*address* and/or at the Belly Buster Burger Bar,_________*address* on or about__*date* , and at the wedding reception of my niece, on or__*date* . Particulars of the Respondent's acts of physical cruelty are as follows:

Example:

Without provocation and for no apparent reason the Respondent would frequently become enraged and verbally abusive towards me. The Respondent would find fault with all sorts of trivialities and would criticize me and demean me in the most sarcastic way possible. The Respondent would do this in public, such as in restaurants and at social events. On one recent occasion at the Belly Buster Burger Bar the Respondent suddenly became angry and loudly called me a fat, stupid cow and called across the restaurant to the waitress to keep the burgers coming because this fat cow (meaning me) never fills up. On another recent occasion, on __*date* , at my niece's wedding, the Respondent flew into a tantrum of anger and announced as loudly as possible to all my relatives present that they can have me back as I am no damn use to anyone anyway. On both these occasions I was so embarrassed and humiliated that I had to leave the room in emotional pain which has not yet healed. On both these occasions and on numerous others I could not face the stress and emotional pain of returning to my own home and I stayed overnight with my only friend. I have been completely unable to please or satisfy the Respondent over the past two years. I have become such a nervous wreck that am constantly depressed, frequently cry for no apparent reason, have frequent thoughts of suicide and feel utterly alone and unable to carry on with my job and my daily life. At the insistence of my friend I have recently sought medical assistance and I am now seeing a psychiatrist. Dr. R.U. Better, who is counseling me individually and through group therapy. I am taking the prescription drug __________, which is a mood enhancer and mood stabilizer. I am certain that if I were to continue in the present relationship with the Respondent I would quickly and inevitably become completely incapacitated and unable to cope with my job and with my daily life. Continuing in a relationship with the Respondent is intolerable to me and I am certain it would utterly destroy me emotionally.

4. I have neither forgiven nor condoned the Respondent's act(s) of adultery to this day, nor will I.

5. It would clearly not be appropriate in the circumstances for the court to consider the possibility of the reconciliation of the spouses because of the facts surrounding the cruelty of the Respondent towards the Applicant. It would be intolerable for the Applicant to reconcile with the Respondent and continue the spousal relationship and it would be a clear danger to the health of the Applicant to do so.

6. This Affidavit is made in support of the allegations of adultery in this proceeding and for no improper purpose or delay.

SWORN BEFORE ME at the City of ______________,

in the County/Judicial district of ________________,

this _____ day of __________, 2__.__

Commissioner of oaths or Notary Public

iv-v Alcoholism and Substance Abuse

Because alcoholism and drug abuse are not by themselves grounds for divorce it is unlikely that anyone would ever be presenting evidence proving a condition of dependency unless as a collateral point on the way to proving something else. Example: One might try to prove a condition of alcoholism in order to prove cruelty. Cruelty, of course, is a valid ground for divorce. So proving the alcoholism in order to prove the cruelty could very well be a valid tactic. But since this is a risky tactic and a shaky proof of cruelty, it should not be relied on as the primary proof of the alleged cruelty, but used only as supporting collateral evidence to the main evidence or as a last resort.

An example of how alcoholism might be incorporated into collateral evidence is given in section 4.4.2 above under the topic of Mental Cruelty.

v. Interlocutory Divorce Decree

In different jurisdictions this document is called an Interlocutory Divorce Order, an Interlocutory Divorce Judgment, a Decree Nisi, and an Interim Judgment of Divorce. Whatever it is called, it is the first of a two part set or court orders that make the divorce final and complete.

It is in this first of the two orders that we find all the collateral orders concerning support, the children, the money and the property.

Again, the exact form and layout of this order varies from jurisdiction to jurisdiction, so a check for how the document is laid out in your local jurisdiction is necessary. It is not practical to reproduce the form used in every jurisdiction in North America here.

The party applying for the divorce has the responsibility of preparing this document, having it approved and signed by the court, and serving it where service of this document is ordered.

What follows is the body of a typical Interlocutory Divorce Decree/Decree Nisi of Divorce.

Court

Judge date of hearing

style of cause

(i.e., standard Order heading)

Interlocutory Divorce Order

Upon reading the application of the Applicant in this proceeding for a Divorce, upon hearing the Applicant and the witnesses, upon reviewing all the evidence, in the presence of the Applicant, the Respondent not being present although duly served, as appears from the Affidavit of Service, filed, *(OR: and the Respondent being present in person]*This Honourable Court does hereby Order and Adjudge:

1. The Applicant and the Respondent in this proceeding, who were married on ___*date*___, is hereby dissolved;
2. The Applicant shall have exclusive custody of the following child/children of the marriage: *(List names and birth dates of children.)*
3. The Respondent shall have the right to visit with the children of the marriage as provided for in clause 4 of the Separation Agreement between the parties, dated___*date*___,which clause is hereby incorporated into this judgment by reference;
4. The Respondent shall pay to the Applicant for support the sum of $______per month;
5. The Respondent shall pay to the Applicant for the support of each child of the marriage the sum of $________ per month;
6. Support for the Applicant and for each child of the marriage shall continue as provided in clause 5 of the Separation Agreement between the parties, which clause is hereby incorporated into this judgment by reference;
7. Clauses 6, 7 and 8 of the said Separation Agreement are hereby incorporated into this judgment by reference;
8. The Respondent shall be served with a true copy of this Order at:______*address*______

If applicable:

9. The Applicant having proven to the satisfaction of This Honourable Court urgent circumstances, and undertakings having been files by the Applicant and Respondent not to appeal this decision, the time for appeal is hereby dispensed with *(OR reduced to ten* days) and the Applicant is (then) at liberty to apply for a Judgment *(OR Decree)* Absolute of Divorce.

If applicable:

10. Costs of this proceeding shall be to the Applicant.

____

The Hon. Judge _______________

THIS JUDGMENT BEARS INTEREST at the rate of __________ per cent per year commencing on *(date).*

NOTE: Every version of Interlocutory Divorce Judgment contains some form of Notice to the Respondent, right below the place for the judge's signature, to the effect that the Respondent has a specific amount of time (usually 3 months) in which to appeal the decision of the court if they wish to do so; otherwise the court's decision will become final and binding. Here is a typical example:

THE SPOUSES ARE NOT FREE TO REMARRY FOR 30/60 DAYS AFTER THIS JUDGMENT TAKES EFFECT, AFTER WHICH TIME A CERTIFICATE OF DIVORCE/JUDGMENT ABSOLUTE OF DIVORCE MAY BE OBTAINED FROM THE COURT. IF DURING THAT TIME AN APPEAL IS MADE IT MAY DELAY THE DATE WHEN THE JUDGMENT TAKES EFFECT.

vi Application for Final Divorce Decree/Certificate of Divorce

Again, the Applicant is responsible for making the application for the final Decree (or Judgment) of Divorce and paying the court's application fee. Don't worry, the fee is not going to be too oppressive. It is usually something around $20.00 or $30.00.

Each jurisdiction will have their own form of Application, so again the best advice is to obtain a specimen from the local court clerk's office or legal aid clinic. While you are at it you can find out what the exact fee for an application is in your jurisdiction.

The supporting documents you will need are a new Affidavit of Service, as proof of service of the Interlocutory Judgment, attached to the original Interlocutory Judgment, and an Affidavit in support of the new application, setting out certain facts that the court will be concerned about. It is with these latter two forms that the next two sections deal.

vi-ii Affidavit of Service of Interlocutory Judgment of Divorce

[Style of Cause]

I, ______________________, of the City of ___________________ in the County of __________________, in the Judicial District of_________________, do solemnly declare as follows:

1. I have personal knowledge of the facts deposed to.

2. On or about the ______ day of__________, 2____, I served the Respondent in this proceeding with a true copy of the Interlocutory Judgment of Divorce attached hereto by:

(Choose one:)

a. delivering the same to the said Respondent at _____*address*_____ in

compliance with the Order of This Honourable Court;

b. mailing the same by prepaid ordinary mail to the said Respondent at____*address*____, in compliance with the Order of This Honourable

Court;

c. causing a Notice of the Interlocutory Judgment for Divorce attached hereto as Exhibit "A" to be published _______ times in the newspaper, The Pleasantville Post and Trumpet, in compliance with the Order of This Honourable Court, and a true copy of the said Notice is attached hereto as Exhibit "B".

3. This Affidavit is made for no improper purpose or delay.

SWORN BEFORE ME at the City of_____________,

in the County/Judicial district of _____________,

this______day of____________, 2___.___

Commissioner of oaths

or Notary Public

vi-iii Affidavit of Service of Interlocutory Judgment of Divorce

[Style of Cause]

I, _______________of the City of in the County of ____________, in the Judicial District of _________________, do solemnly declare as follows:

1. I have personal knowledge of the facts deposed to.
2. I have not been served with a Notice of Appeal nor with a notice of any other pleadings or proceedings in connection with this proceeding or any issue deriving from the dissolution of the marriage between the parties hereto or corollary relief granted since this court made the Judgment/Decree of___*date* nor am I aware in fact of any such action or proceeding.
3. The Respondent and I have not reconciled.
4. This Affidavit is made in support of an application for a Judgment Absolute/Final Judgment/Decree Absolute of Divorce in this proceeding and for no improper purpose.

SWORN BEFORE ME at the City of_____________,

in the County/Judicial district of _____________,

this______day of____________, 2___.___

Commissioner of oaths

or Notary Public

Getting Around Some Obstacles

4.GETTING AROUND SOME OBSTACLES

Sometimes it is not possible to comply with a rule of procedure and therefore the divorce proceeding is stalled. These are times when a Motion is required to obtain a judge's special solution or special permission to vary the rule as it is set down. What follows are some common examples of these kinds of special circumstances and the Motions that are used to fix the problems.

(1) Respondent's Whereabouts Unknown or Respondent Is In Hiding

The situation of the husband or wife who has simply disappeared is really quite common. Sometimes a person just wants to escape from a bad relationship and make a new, clean start. Sometimes a person wants to hide from their responsibilities.

Divorce regulations throughout North America require that divorce pleadings (i.e. documents) must be served on the Respondent in person. This is called personal service. Service in any other form is called substituted service. Personal service is what the basic requirement is.

Where a judge is satisfied that personal service is not possible, the next best choice is unanimously seen to be service on a relative or some person who is known to still be in regular communication with the Respondent.

Where service on a person in contact with the Respondent is not possible because no such person is known, the next best choice is publication in a widely circulated newspaper in a municipal area where the Respondent was last known to be.

Substitutes service by newspaper is followed by one more alternative, which many judges are quite hesitant to use except in the most compelling of circumstances:

completely dispensing with service of pleadings.

There is also the possibility of service at the last known address of the Respondent by ordinary mail. There must be some evidence that the Respondent is likely to return to that address for a judge to make such an order. Otherwise it is pretty much a waste of time and the judges know it. Besides, if the Respondent is likely to return, what is wrong with personal service? So, substituted service at a last known address, as it is called, is frowned on by most of the judiciary, and is used only sparingly. But don't rule it out entirely; I have found it useful in cases where I had to serve a travelling salesman, or when I knew the Respondent's address but it was clear that the Respondent was just being uncooperative after several attempts at service and was evading service to cause delay.

(1.1) Motion for Substituted Service/Dispensing With Service

This is a typical example of how personal service is changed to substituted service by making a Motion, in this case, to a judge in chambers.

[Style of Cause]

Notice of Motion for Substituted Service

The Respondent will make a Motion to a judge in chambers on _ *date* at 9:30 a.m., or so soon thereafter as the Motion can be heard, at the court house, *address* , *Chambers Room*

The Motion is to be heard:

- ☐ in writing and; on consent; unopposed; made without notice;
- ☐ in writing and opposed;
- ☐ orally.

The Motion is for an Order dispensing with service of the divorce pleadings and proceedings on the Respondent.

Alternatively, the Motion is for an Order that the Respondent be served with a Notice of this proceeding by publication 3 times in the Classified Legal Notices Section, of the newspaper, the Pleasantville Post and Trumpet, and this shall be good, valid and sufficient service of the Respondent for the purposes of this proceeding.

The grounds for this Motion are that the whereabouts of the Respondent have been unknown for the past _____ months/years and cannot now be discovered, despite the best efforts of the Applicant to do so.

The following documentary evidence will be used at the hearing of this Motion:

a. The Affidavit of the Applicant, filed herewith, in support of this Motion;

b. An extract from the Pleasantville telephone directory, attached as an exhibit to the said Affidavit of the Applicant, showing no listing for the Respondent;

c. A letter on the letterhead of the Pleasantville Telephone Company, signed by ____________, Chief Records Supervisor, attached as an exhibit to the said Affidavit of the Applicant, to the effect that there is no telephone listing for the Respondent as recently as 7 days prior to this Motion;

d. A print out from the Applicant's computer search of the national telephone listings of Canada and the United States, attached as an exhibit to the said Affidavit of the Applicant, showing all the listings for the same name and for the same first initial plus surname as the Respondent, none of which are actually the Respondent, as recently as 2 days prior to this Motion;

e. The pleadings and proceedings herein;

f. Such further or other documents, materials and evidence as the Applicant may present and this Hon. Court may permit.

(Note: The last two items are routinely inserted to allow for last minute insertions and additions at the hearing not previously anticipated.)

<u>date</u> (Name, address, phone no., fax no. of the Applicant)

TO: the Clerk of this Hon. Court

(1.2) Affidavit Supporting Motion for Substituted Service

[Style of Cause]

Affidavit in Support of Motion

I, the Applicant in this proceeding, make oath and say as follows:

1. I have personal knowledge of the facts deposed to herein.

2. I have not been in contact nor have I heard from or about the Respondent for the past ______ months/years.

3. I have attempted to contact the Respondent by telephoning the only cousin of the Respondent that I know of. She has indicated that she has not heard from the Respondent for at least the same length of time. She and I have always gotten along well and I have no reason not to believe her.

4. I have attempted to contact the Respondent by telephoning the Respondent's mother, only parent of the Respondent still living. She has indicated that she has not heard from the Respondent for at least the same length of time. She and I have always gotten along well and I have no reason not to believe her.

5. I have attempted to contact the Respondent by telephoning the Respondent's only two close friends, the only friends with whom there is any chance of continued contact. They have indicated that they have not heard from the Respondent for at least the same length of time as me. They and I have always gotten along well and I have no reason not to believe them.

6. I have attempted and failed to find the Respondent's whereabouts by the following searches:

   i. telephone directory for this community, see true copy, exhibit "A";
   ii. Pleasantville Telephone Company special search, under the authority of the Supervisor of Customer Listings, see letter of confirmation, exhibit "B";
   iii. national telephone listings for Canada and the United States via internet search, see true copy of computer print out, exhibit "C";
   iv. Drivers licence record search for this jurisdiction, see search results certificate, exhibit "D".

7. I have contacted a private investigator who performs skip trace searches to locate people, but I can not afford his rate, especially since he indicates that there is no guarantee if and when a positive match may occur, if at all. I have myself and three children to support and a house mortgage payment to maintain, in addition to other living expenses, and only my job to support me, with no help from anyone. This is an expense that would seriously impair my ability to meet my financial obligations.

8. In view of the circumstances, where the Respondent has made no effort to keep in touch, but has rather chosen to disappear, and where the Respondent has shown no continuing interest even in his own family and friends, and in view of my circumstances, I think it would be appropriate for this

Hon. Court to order that service of the notice and pleadings and proceedings herein be dispensed with entirely.

9. Alternatively, if this Hon. Court finds it inappropriate to dispense with service, I think it would also be appropriate for this Hon. Court to order that the Respondent be served with the Notice and pleadings and proceedings herein by publication of a Notice in the Classified legal Section of the Pleasantville Post and Trumpet on one/three occasion(s) and that such publication shall be good, sufficient and valid service on the Respondent.

10. This Affidavit is made in support of the Motion filed herewith and for no improper purpose or delay.

SWORN BEFORE ME at the City of________________

in the county of _____________, this________day of

_____________, 2____.____

A commissioner of oaths or notary public

(1.3) Order for Substituted Service

(Choose and insert either no. i or no. 2, below. Have your draft Order ready when you submit your Motion and Affidavit. You will be asked for it. If you are unsure which the judge will decide on, prepare 2 alternate Orders and pull out the right one when asked.)

The Hon. Judge __________ _____day, the _____day of _____,2 _____.

[Style of Cause]

Order for Dispensing With/Substituted Service

Upon the application of the Applicant, upon reading the Motion and Affidavit, filed, upon reading the pleadings and proceedings herein, and upon hearing the Applicant, the Respondent not appearing, this court hereby orders:

I. Service of the notice and pleadings and proceedings herein is hereby dispensed with;

II. The Respondent shall be served with the notice and pleadings and proceedings herein by publication of a Notice in the Classified legal Section of the Pleasantville Post and Trumpet on one/three occasion(s) and that such publication shall be good, sufficient and valid service on the Respondent.

III. Costs shall be costs in the cause.

____

Judge

(2) Dealing With the Legally Mentally Incompetent Respondent

A person who is or who has become mentally incompetent in the eyes of the law can not be expected to understand or appreciate what a divorce proceeding is or the consequences and effects of getting divorced. Why? Because they are not mentally rational. Therefore all jurisdictions have special arrangements in place to protect those with mental disorders from being taken advantage of. If you must deal with or serve notice on a Respondent who is or has become mentally incompetent there is a special step you must take before you are permitted to proceed.

The special provision you must observe is not too troublesome. It is merely a form of substituted service. But you need to know about it so as not to run into delay and embarrassment.

A typical solution to this situation appears in the following section

(2.1) Motion for Sustituted Service on a Guardian or The Official Guardian

Note: The Official Guardian, mentioned below, is a kind of ombudsman, a government official whose job it is to intervene in legal proceedings to protect the rights and assets of children, deceased persons, persons in psychiatric institutions, and certain others who can not be expected to protect themselves and who have no one else to turn to for protection.

[Style of Cause]

Notice of Motion for Substituted Service

On the Chief Administrator of Happy Haven Psychiatric Hospital

Or on the Official Guardian

The Respondent will make a Motion to a judge in chambers on ___*date*___ at 9:30 a.m., or so soon thereafter as the Motion can be heard, at the court house,_ ___*address*___, ___*Chambers Room*___

The Motion is to be heard:

- ☐ in writing and; on consent; unopposed; made without notice;
- ☐ in writing and opposed;
- ☐ orally.

The Motion is for an Order that the Respondent be served with a Notice of this proceeding by delivery of a true copy of the pleadings and proceedings herein to the Chief Administrator of Happy Haven Psychiatric Hospital at ___*address*___

(*OR* to the Official Guardian at ___*address*___), who appears to be the person having care, custody and control over the affairs of the Respondent, and this shall be good, valid and sufficient service of the Respondent for the purposes of this proceeding.

The grounds for this Motion are that the Respondent has been a voluntary/involuntary patient of the said psychiatric facility for the past ________ months/years and cannot now be served, except through a guardian who will represent the Applicant.

The following documentary evidence will be used at the hearing of this Motion:

1. The Affidavit of the Applicant, filed herewith, in support of this Motion;

2. A letter on the letterhead of the Happy Haven Psychiatric Hospital, signed by __________, Chief Records Officer, attached as an exhibit to the said Affidavit of the Applicant, to the effect that the Respondent is in fact presently a patient there;

3. The pleadings and proceedings herein;

4. Such further or other documents, materials and evidence as the

Applicant may present and this Hon. Court may permit.

(Note: The last two items are routinely inserted to allow for last minute insertions and additions at the hearing not previously anticipated.)

date *(Name, address, phone no., fax no. of the Applicant)*

TO: the Clerk of this Hon. Court

AND TO: Mr.

Chief Administrator,

Happy Haven Psychiatric Hospital

address

(OR)

The Official Guardian

address

(1.2) Affidavit Supporting Motion for Substituted Service

[Style of Cause]

Affidavit in Support of Motion for Substituted Service

I, the Applicant in this proceeding, make oath and say as follows:

1. I have personal knowledge of the facts deposed to herein.
2. The Respondent has been a voluntary/involuntary patient of the Happy Haven Psychiatric Hospital for the past ______ months/years and cannot now be served, except through a guardian who will represent the Applicant.
3. The Chief Administrator of the Happy Haven Psychiatric Hospital *(OR* the Official Guardian, as *the case may be)* appears to be the only person having any right to or obligation for the care, custody and control over the affairs of the Respondent.
4. Attached hereto as an exhibit is a letter on the letterhead of the Happy Haven Psychiatric Hospital, signed by _______, Chief Records Officer, to the effect that the Respondent is in fact presently a patient there.

5. This Affidavit is made in support of the Motion filed herewith and for no improper purpose or delay.

SWORN BEFORE ME at the City of________________

in the county of ______________, this_________day of

_______________, 2___. ___

A commissioner of oaths or notary public

public (1.3) Order for Substituted Service

(Have your draft Order ready when you submit your Motion and Affidavit. You will be asked for it.)

The Hon. Judge __________ _____day, the _____day of _____,2 _____.

[Style of Cause]

Order for Substituted Service on Guardian

Upon the application of the Applicant, upon reading the Motion and Affidavit, filed, upon reading the pleadings and proceedings herein, and upon hearing the Applicant, no one appearing for the Respondent, although duly served with the Notice of Motion and Affidavit herein, this court hereby orders:

1. The Respondent shall be served with the notice and pleadings and proceedings herein, along with a true copy of this Order, by service on the Chief

Administrator of the Happy Haven Psychiatric Hospital/ Official Guardian at ____*address*______ and such service shall be good, sufficient and valid service on the Respondent.

2. Costs shall be costs in the cause.

____

Judge

(3) The Matrimonial Home When Who Stays and Who Leaves Cannot Be Decided

Sometimes both spouses want to remain in the matrimonial home. Both continue to live there and encounter one another every day. The situation is awkward at best, certainly uncomfortable for both, probably stressful, likely the source of strong feelings and perhaps expressions of anger, and, in the worst case, a downright dangerous situation. It is a situation to be frowned on, discouraged, avoided

I have seen situations on some rare occasions where spouses have lived completely separate lives under the same roof in relative harmony. Some judges find it suspicious when a couple share the same residence and yet seek a divorce, claiming that they cannot live together. Such suspicions may even lead these judges to deny the divorce if the submissions are not overwhelmingly convincing.

There is no longer a legal advantage to being the one who is "abandoned", just as there is no stigma and no penalty attached to being the one who moves out first, anywhere in North America.

The only argument that I have ever heard that makes any sense to me in support of staying in the matrimonial home is the argument that the cost of moving plus the cost of first and last month's rent is more than a spouse can afford.

When spouses simply can not agree as to who should make the initial move and move out, then it is up to the court to make the decision. This is to be avoided if possible, because the court may impose terms that neither spouse is happy with. That is the risk of placing the power of decision in the hands of an outside person. But if you must follow this route, here, on the following pages, is a typical way of handling this situation.

(3.1) Notice of Motion for Exclusive Possession of Matrimonial Home. Interim Custody. Interim Support

(Choose only those clauses following and parts of clauses that apply to your situation.)

[Style of Cause]

Notice of Motion for Exclusive Possession of Matrimonial Home, Interim Custody, and Interim Support

(Choose only those clauses following and parts of clauses that apply to your situation.)

The Respondent will make a Motion to a judge in chambers on *date___* at 9:30 a.m., or so soon thereafter as the Motion can be heard, at the court house, *___address_______. Chambers Room*

The Motion is to be heard:

- ☐ in writing and; on consent; unopposed; made without notice;
- ☐ in writing and opposed;
- ☐ orally.

The Motion is for an Order that the Applicant has exclusive possession of the matrimonial home for him/herself *(if applicable, and for the children of the marriage),* effective immediately.

The Motion is further for an Order that the Respondent shall pay one half the mortgage payments and property taxes in the interim until the matter is further and more fully dealt with in the full hearing of this proceeding.

The grounds for this Motion are that the Respondent has been a severe and intolerable source of stress and contention for the Applicant and the children of the marriage and it is intolerable to them to continue living with the Respondent under the present living arrangements, and further that it is more convenient, more reasonable and less disruptive for the Respondent to move out that it would be for the Applicant and children to move out.

The following documentary evidence will be used at the hearing of this Motion:

I. The Affidavit of the Applicant, filed herewith, in support of this Motion;

2. The pleadings and proceedings herein;

3. Such further or other documents, materials and evidence as the Applicant may present and this Hon. Court may permit.

(Note: The last item is routinely inserted to allow for last minute insertions and additions at the hearing not previously anticipated.)

____date____ *(Name, address, phone no., fax no. of the Applicant)*

TO: the Clerk of this Hon. Court

AND TO: Mr.

Chief Administrator,

Happy Haven Psychiatric Hospital
_____*address*_____

(OR)

The Official Guardian

_____*address*_____

(1.2) Affidavit Supporting Motion for Exclusive Possession of the Matrimonial Home. Interim Custody. Interim Support

(Choose only those clauses following and parts of clauses that apply to your situation.)

[Style of Cause]

Affidavit in Support of Motion for

Exclusive Possession of the Matrimonial Home

I, the Applicant in this proceeding, make oath and say as follows:

1. I have personal knowledge of the facts deposed to herein.

2. The Respondent and I have been living entirely separate and apart, living separate lives, since or about *date* . But we have been sharing the same physical facilities at our residence, our last matrimonial home, at _____*address*_____, save and except for sleeping arrangements.

(If applicable)

3. The Respondent and I have been unable to agree on terms of maintaining and supporting financially two separate residences, despite our best efforts, and we seem to have come to an impasse.

(If applicable)

4. The Respondent and I have been unable to agree on terms of child custody and visiting rights, despite our best efforts to come to an agreement and we seem to be at an impasse. The issues in clauses 3 and 4 will have to be dealt with at length by this Hon. Court, but in the interim the children appear content to remain with me in the matrimonial home and the Respondent has made no other interim provision or arrangement for their interim custody, care and control.

5. On several occasions the Respondent and I had such seriously heated arguments that the Respondent threatened to become physically abusive and harm me and even to kill me. I have always preferred to regard these verbal threats as made in the heat of the moment and not meant seriously. But on two separate occasions I have sustained hard slaps about the face. I know the Respondent well, we being married. These days of high stress and feelings of near constant anger make me concerned that the Respondent may just be on the verge of snapping and acting out all those feelings of tension by becoming physically abusive. The children and I feel in imminent danger of physical abuse.

6. I repeat and incorporate by reference the grounds for divorce in this proceeding. The marriage has completely broken down and we are unable to cooperate and agree on even the simplest issues of ordinary living. The home situation is an environment of anger, hostility, constant argument, disrespect, confrontation, high stress and depression. A prime cause of the bad home environment is the Respondent and the friction he/she creates when he/she is present, both with me and with the children. When the Respondent is absent virtually all the bad atmosphere disappears and the children and I enjoy an atmosphere of tranquility and cooperation.

7. My family physician has referred me to Dr.______*name*______ for psychological counseling and I am taking ______*name*______ , a prescription tranquilizer medication for my nerves, and I really believe that I should seek a period of care in a psychiatric hospital, but I am trying to keep going because the children depend on me. I am confident that my symptoms would improve dramatically if the Respondent would move into a separate residence.

8. The Respondent seems content to share the physical facilities of the matrimonial home with me (us) indefinitely and has shown no inclination to establish a separate residence.

9. The home situation has become intolerable for me and I also fear it is going to be a source of emotional trauma and the cause of future therapy for the children. I do not wish to expose the children, and myself, to such a harmful home environment.

10. If I could afford to move out of the matrimonial home with the children I would do so immediately. If I thought that another residence were equally suitable for the children's school, after-school activities and social lives, I would change residences immediately, even if it meant making some financial sacrifices. But I am not able to find a comparable residence that is about equally suitable for the needs and comfort of the children at a price that I can afford. Nor can I stay in the same residence with the children without the financial assistance of the Respondent, as my financial statements, filed, show.

11. Since we also can not agree on an appropriate amount of financial support for the Respondent to pay to me as interim support and for the maintenance of the Respondent's half of the matrimonial home, I am also seeking the intervention of this Hon. Court to set an appropriate amount in the interim, until a more thorough review can be made in this proceeding.

12. This Affidavit is made in support of the Motion filed herewith and for no improper purpose or delay.

SWORN BEFORE ME at the City of________________

in the county of _____________, this________day of

______________, 2______. ______

A commissioner of oaths or notary public

(1.3) Order for Exclusive Possession of the Matrimonial Home

(Have your draft Order ready when you submit your Motion and Affidavit. You will be asked for it.)

The Hon. Judge __________ _____day, the _____day of _____,2 _____.

[Style of Cause]

Order for Exclusive Possession of the Matrimonial Home.

Interim Custody and Interim Support

(Choose only those clauses following and parts of clauses that apply to your situation.)

Upon the application of the Applicant, upon reading the Motion and Applicant's Affidavit, filed, upon reading the pleadings and proceedings herein, and upon hearing the Applicant, no one appearing for the Respondent, although duly served with the Notice of Motion and Affidavit herein:

1. This Court Orders that the Applicant shall have exclusive possession of the matrimonial home along with the children of the marriage, effective as of____*date*____.
2. This Court further orders that the Applicant shall have exclusive care, custody and control of the following children of the marriage:

   (Name the children and their birth dates')
3. This Court further orders that the Respondent shall have unrestricted access to visit the children of the marriage outside the matrimonial home on giving 24 hours notice of intention to visit and it not being detrimental to the well-being of the children or their schedules to do so.
4. This Court further Orders and adjudges that beginning the first of the month next following this Order, the Respondent shall pay to the Applicant as support for the maintenance of the matrimonial home one half of the mortgage payments, one half of the property taxes, one half of the cost of any painting, roof repair, building repair, electrical or plumbing repair bill. The Applicant shall be entirely responsible for all utility and telephone account charges, including hydro, water, gas and cable television bills, appliance, furnace and central air conditioning maintenance and common maintenance expenses under $200.00.
5. This Court further orders that the Respondent, upon giving 24 hours notice to the Applicant, and if the time is mutually convenient to both, may enter the matrimonial home to remove any belongings mutually agreed to belong to the Respondent.

6. Respondent shall be served with a true copy of this Order.

7. Costs shall be costs in the cause.

____

Judge

PARENTING GUIDE

The Parenting Guide is designed to help you co-parent within the context of divorce and is designed to help parents working together on a parenting agreement.

The forms are designed to hold the most important information about your child(ren) – school, doctor, dentist, optician etc.

1. Child Info
2. Contacts
3. Emergency Info
4. Holiday Schedule
5. Support Payment Log
6. Child Expenses 1-7
7. Parent/Child Activities
8. Activity Calendar
9. School & Extra Curricular Activity
10. Activities List
11. Family & Friends Timetable
12. Phone Calls with Children
13. Weekly Phone Log
14. Photographs
15. Safety Checklist
16. Parenting Schedule
17. Parenting Letters
18. Phone Calls
19. Incident Report
20. Child Behaviour & Log

DISCLAIMER

The material contained here is not Legal Advice and is to be used to help parents with parenting issues during/after divorce.

Child Info

SELF HELP
Step by Step Divorce
& Parenting Guide

TODAY'S DATE: ______________

Name ______________

Date ______________

D/O/B ______________

SIN# ______________

School ______________

Teacher ______________

Principal ______________

School Phone ______________

School Fax ______________

Doctor ______________

Doctor Phone ______________

Doctor Fax ______________

Blood Type ______________

Identifying Birth Marks ______________

Photo

Photo Date ______________

Age of Child ______________

Child's Signature

Thumb Print

Finger Prints (Left Hand)

Thumb Print

Finger Prints (Right Hand)

Contacts

SELF HELP

Step By Step Divorce, Separation Agreement & Parenting Guide

PARENTING GUIDE

The Parenting Guide is designed to help you co-parent within the context of divorce and is designed to help parents working together on a parenting agreement.

The forms are designed to hold the most important information about your child(ren) – school, doctor, dentist, optician etc.

1. Child Info
2. Contacts
3. Emergency Info
4. Holiday Schedule
5. Support Payment Log
6. Child Expenses 1-7
7. Parent/Child Activities
8. Activity Calendar
9. School & Extra Curricular Activity
10. Activities List
11. Family & Friends Timetable
12. Phone Calls with Children
13. Weekly Phone Log
14. Photographs
15. Safety Checklist
16. Parenting Schedule
17. Parenting Letters
18. Phone Calls
19. Incident Report
20. Child Behaviour & Log

DISCLAIMER

The material contained here is not Legal Advice and is to be used to help parents with parenting issues during/after divorce.

Child Info

SELF HELP
Step by Step Divorce
& Parenting Guide

TODAY'S DATE: ____________

Name ____________

Date ____________

D/O/B ____________

SIN# ____________

School ____________

Teacher ____________

Principal ____________

School Phone ____________

School Fax ____________

Doctor ____________

Doctor Phone ____________

Doctor Fax ____________

Blood Type ____________

Identifying Birth Marks ____________

Photo

Photo Date ____________

Age of Child ____________

Child's Signature

Thumb Print

Finger Prints (Left Hand)

Thumb Print

Finger Prints (Right Hand)

Contacts

SELF HELP
Step By Step Divorce, Separation Agreement & Parenting Guide

Other Parent ____________________
Legal Name ____________________
Address ____________________
____
____
Res ( ) ________ Cell ( ) ________
Off ( ) ________ Fax ( ) ________
Alternate Phone No. ( ) ____________________
Notes ____________________
____
____
____
____

Maternal Relatives ____________________
Name ____________________
Address ____________________
____
____
Res ( ) ________ Off ( ) ________
Alternate Phone No. ( ) ____________________
Notes ____________________
____
____

Name ____________________
Address ____________________
____
____
Res ( ) ________ Off ( ) ________
Alternate Phone No. ( ) ____________________
Notes ____________________
____
____

School ____________________
Name ____________________
Address ____________________
____
____
Off ( ) ________ Fax ( ) ________
Principal ____________________
Home Rm. Teacher ____________________
Alternate Teacher ____________________
Gym / Coach ____________________
Guidance Counselor ____________________
Secretary ____________________
Classroom No. ____________________

Paternal Relatives ____________________
Name ____________________
Address ____________________
____
____
Res ( ) ________ Off ( ) ________
Alternate Phone No. ( ) ____________________
Notes ____________________
____
____

Name ____________________
Address ____________________
____
____
Res ( ) ________ Off ( ) ________
Alternate Phone No. ( ) ____________________
Notes ____________________
____
____

Contacts 2

SELF HELP
Step By Step Divorce, Separation Agreement & Parenting Guide

Best Friend 1 ______
Name of Friend ______
Parents Name ______
Address ______
______
Res ( ) ______
______

Best Friend 2 ______
Name of Friend ______
Parents Name ______
Address ______
______
Res ( ) ______

Boyfriend / Girlfriend ______
Name of Friend ______
Parents Name ______
Address ______
______
Off ( ) ______
______

Notes ______
______
______
______
______
______

Activities

Sport 1 ______
Coach ______
Address of Activity ______
______
Tel ( ) ______
Notes ______
______
______

Sport 2 ______
Coach ______
Address of Activity ______
______
Tel ( ) ______
Notes ______
______
______

Memberships ______
Program Leader ______
Address of Activity ______
______
Tel ( ) ______
Notes ______
______
______
______
______

Camp ______
Counselor ______
Address of Activity ______
______
Tel ( ) ______
Notes ______
______
______
______
______

Emergency Info

SELF HELP
Step By Step Divorce, Separation Agreement & Parenting Guide

Pediatrician
Name
Address

Off ( ) Fax ( )
Pgr ( )
After Hours ( )
Patient Since:
Notes

Doctor
Name
Address

Off ( ) Fax ( )
Pgr ( )
After Hours ( )
Patient Since:
Notes

Dentist
Name
Address

Off ( ) Fax ( )
Pgr ( )
After Hours ( )
Patient Since:
Notes

Orthodontist
Name
Address

Off ( ) Fax ( )
Pgr ( )
After Hours ( )
Patient Since:
Notes

Specialist
Name
Address

Off ( ) Fax ( )
Pgr ( )
After Hours ( )
Patient Since:
Notes

Optician
Name
Address

Off ( ) Fax ( )
Pgr ( )
After Hours ( )
Patient Since:
Notes

Emergency Info

SELF HELP
Step By Step Divorce, Separation Agreement & Parenting Guide

Other Professional ____________________
Name ____________________
Address ____________________
____
____
Off ( ) Fax ( )
Pgr ( )
After Hours ( )
Patient Since:
Notes

Other Professional ____________________
Name ____________________
Address ____________________
____
____
Off ( ) Fax ( )
Pgr ( )
After Hours ( )
Patient Since:
Notes

OTHER EMERGENCY PHONE NUMBERS

DIAL 911 - IF AVAILABLE IN YOUR COMMUNITY

Fire Department ____________________ Tel ( )

Ambulance ____________________ Tel ( )

Poison Controa Center ____________________ Tel ( )

Hospital ____________________ Tel ( )

Veterinarian ____________________ Tel ( )

Water Company ____________________ Tel ( )

Gas Company ____________________ Tel ( )

Electric Company ____________________ Tel ( )

Oil Company ____________________ Tel ( )

Special Days Holiday Schedual

SELF HELP
Step By Step Divorce, Separation Agreement & Parenting Guide

Name of Child ______________________ D/O/B ______________________

Holiday / Event	Arrival Date and Time	Departure Date and Time	at Dad's Home	at Mom's Home
Child's Birthday				
Dad's Birthday Day				
Mom's Birthday Day				
Mother's Day				
Father's Day				
March Break				
Easter				
Victoria Day Wknd				
July 1 Wknd				
Civic Holiday Wknd				
Labor Day Wknd				
Thanksgiving				
Halloween				

Special Days Holiday Schedual 2

SELF HELP
Step By Step Divorce, Separation Agreement & Parenting Guide

Name of Child ____________________ D/O/B ____________________

Holiday / Event	Arrival Date and Time	Departure Date and Time	at Dad's Home	at Mom's Home
Remembrance Day				
Christmas Eve				
Christmas Day				
New Year's Eve/Day				
Hannukah				
Yom Kippur				
Purim				
Passover				
VACATIONS				
Summer				
Winter				
Spring				
Other				

Support Log

SELF HELP
Step By Step Divorce, Separation Agreement & Parenting Guide

Support payments for the year of ______________________ Page No. ______________

Date Due	Amount Due	Date of Payment	Check Number	Amount Paid	Balance Due

Child Expenses 1

COURT TACTIC-SELF HELP

Step by Step Divorce, Separation Agreement & Parenting Guide

This Tracking system can form the basis of discussions to ascertain the expenses involved in raising your Child(ren).

COMMUNICATIONS	JAN	FEB	MAR	APR	MAY	JUN	JUL	AUG	SEP	OCT	NOV	DEC
Private telephone for kids												
Long distance costs												
800 phone line												
Voice-mailbox												
e-mail/Internet access												
EDUCATION												
Nursery school												
Private school tuition/fees												
Private school uniforms												
Private school room/board												
Other school tuition & fees												
Other school uniforms												
Other school room & board												
College tuition												
University tuition												
Books												
Supplies												
Gifts												
Travel												
Insurance												
Religious donations												

Child Expenses 2

COURT TACTIC-SELF HELP

Step by Step Divorce, Separation Agreement & Parenting Guide

This Tracking system can form the basis of discussions to ascertain the expenses involved in raising your Child(ren).

EDUCATION	JAN	FEB	MAR	APR	MAY	JUN	JUL	AUG	SEP	OCT	NOV	DEC	TOTAL
Tutoring													
Special Education													
Sport uniforms													
Other 1													
Other 2													
Other 3													
Other 4													
Other 5													
ENTERTAINMENT													
Restaurant													
Movies													
Video Rentals													
Theatre													
Concerts													

Child Expenses 3

COURT TACTIC-SELF HELP

Step by Step Divorce, Separation Agreement & Parenting Guide

This Tracking system can form the basis of discussions to ascertain the expenses involved in raising your Child(ren).

GIFTS	JAN	FEB	MAR	APR	MAY	JUN	JUL	AUG	SEP	OCT	NOV	DEC	TOTAL
Birthdays/friends													
Birthday's family													
Christmas													
Valentine's day													
Easter													
Other 1													
Other 2													
Other 3													
Other 4													
Other 5													
Weddings													
Anniversaries													
Baby showers													
Graduations/Scholarships													
Final Sporting Events													
Recitals													
Greeting cards													
Gift wrap etc.													
Miscellaneous													
HOUSING													
Room costs/Housing													

Child Expenses 4

COURT TACTIC-SELF HELP
Step by Step Divorce, Separation Agreement & Parenting Guide

This Tracking system can form the basis of discussions to ascertain the expenses involved in raising your Child(ren).

MAJOR PURCHASES	JAN	FEB	MAR	APR	MAY	JUN	JUL	AUG	SEP	OCT	NOV	DEC	TOTAL
Furniture													
Carpets													
Appliances													
TV/VCR													
Computer													
Car													
Motocycle													
Moutain Bicycle													
Stereo													
MEDICAL													
Hospital/Doctor													
Dentist													
Orthodontist													
Specialists													
Psychologists													
Deductible fees/insurance													
Over the counter medication													
Prescription													
Lab fees													
Special test													
Eyeglasses													

Child Expenses
5

COURT TACTIC-SELF HELP
Step by Step Divorce, Separation Agreement & Parenting Guide

This Tracking system can form the basis of discussions to ascertain the expenses involved in raising your Child(ren).

MEDICAL Continued	JAN	FEB	MAR	APR	MAY	JUN	JUL	AUG	SEP	OCT	NOV	DEC	TOTAL
Hearing aids													
First aid suppliesProsthesis													
Misc. Medical supplies													
Other 1													
Other 2													
Other 3													
MISCELLANEOUS													
Childcare													
Babysitters													
Clothing													
Allowances													
Special events													
Recreation/Sports													
Membership dues/fees													
Parties Birthday's/Holidays													
Costumes(plays, special event)													
Halloween													
Books													
School supplies													
Misc. supplies													

Child Expenses
6

COURT TACTIC-SELF HELP
Step by Step Divorce, Separation Agreement & Parenting Guide

This Tracking system can form the basis of discussions to ascertain the expenses involved in raising your Child(ren).

MISCELLANEOUS	JAN	FEB	MAR	APR	MAY	JUN	JUL	AUG	SEP	OCT	NOV	DEC	TOTAL
Lessons (Music etc.)													
Travel													
Summer Camp													
Vehicles - Maintainance													
Vehicles - Repair													
Stationary													
Stamps													
Toys													
Tapes													
CD's													
Toiletries													
Hairdresser/ Barber													
Cable TV													
Internet access													
Pets													
Pocket money/Allowance													
Sports related items													
PROFESSIONAL SERVICES													
Financial planner													
Accountant													
Lawyer													

Child Expenses
7

COURT TACTIC-SELF HELP

Step by Step Divorce, Separation Agreement & Parenting Guide

This Tracking system can form the basis of discussions to ascertain the expenses involved in raising your Child(ren).

REPAIR ANDSERVICES	JAN	FEB	MAR	APR	MAY	JUN	JUL	AUG	SEP	OCT	NOV	DEC	TOTAL
Electrical/Plumbing													
Painting/ Wall Paper													
Carpet/Window/Cleaning Services													
COMMUNICATIONS													
EDUCATION													
ENTERTAINMENT													
FOOD													
GIFTS													
HOUSING													
MAJOR PURCHASES													
MEDICAL													
MISCELLANEOUS													
PROFESSIONAL SERVICES													
REPAIRS AND SERVICES													
SUPPORT PAYMENTS													
TRANSPORTATION													

Parent/Child Activities

COURT TACTIX-SELF HELP

Step by Step Divorce, Separation Agreement & Parenting Guide

MONTH ________________YEAR________________

SUNDAY	MONDAY	TUESDAY	WEDNESDAY	THURSDAY	FRIDAY	SATURSDAY

Instructions:
On this sheet, track or plan those times during the month that you and your child(ren) did some- thing one-on-one or as a family if there ismore than one child.

Date Activity Cancelled	Reason Given	Re-Scheduled?

Activity Calendar

COURT TACTIX-SELF HELP
Step by Step Divorce, Separation Agreement & Parenting Guide

MONTH ________________YEAR________________

SUNDAY	MONDAY	TUESDAY	WEDNESDAY	THURSDAY	FRIDAY	SATURSDAY

HIGHLIGHT DATES/TIMES WHEN SCHEDULED ACTIVITIES WERE CANCELLED

Examples: Clubs Teams and Sports That are not school organized.
- See Activities List Refer to the School & Extra Curricular Sheet for School-Related activities.

Date Activity Cancelled	Reason Given

School &
Extra Curricular

COURT TACTIX-SELF HELP

Step by Step Divorce, Separation
Agreement & Parenting Guide

MONTH ________________YEAR________________

SUNDAY	MONDAY	TUESDAY	WEDNESDAY	THURSDAY	FRIDAY	SATURSDAY

HIGHLIGHT DATES/TIMES WHEN SCHEDULED ACTIVITIES WERE CANCELLED

Examples:

- PTA meetings
- Class outings
- Parents Night and other school activities
- Car pooling
- Parent/Teacher meetings

Date Activity Cancelled	Reason Given

School &
Extra Curricular

COURT TACTIX-SELF HELP
Step by Step Divorce, Separation Agreement & Parenting Guide

FOR THE WEEK OF ________________YEAR________________

How to use this Form

Check off the activities that apply for this week. Enter this data and notes into the activity calendars as appropriate

Household Chores

- ☐ Do Dishes
- ☐ Empty garbage
- ☐ Laundry
- ☐ Make Beds
- ☐ Make Meals
- ☐ Clean rooms
- ☐ Recycling
- ☐ Vacuum
- ☐ Shopping
- ☐ Others

____

____

Routine Activities

- ☐ Breakfast, Lunch
- ☐ Dinner/ Family
- ☐ Time-talking
- ☐ Hygiene- baths,
- ☐ Showers, brush
- ☐ teeth, comb hair
- ☐ Walk to school
- ☐ Drive to school
- ☐ Bus to school
- ☐ Meet for lunch
- ☐ Bedtime story
- ☐ Watch TV together
- ☐ Others

____

____

Clubs and Team Sports (Not School)

- ☐ Art-draw, paint, Cut and paste
- ☐ Basketball
- ☐ Biking
- ☐ Camping
- ☐ Crafts
- ☐ Exercising
- ☐ Hiking
- ☐ Hockey
- ☐ Jogging
- ☐ Martial arts
- ☐ Sailing
- ☐ Skating
- ☐ Soccer
- ☐ T-Ball
- ☐ Tennis
- ☐ Tobogganing
- ☐ Observing wildlife-
- ☐ Others

Extra Curricular School

- ☐ Art-draw, paint,Cut and paste
- ☐ Basketball
- ☐ Biking
- ☐ Camping
- ☐ Crafts
- ☐ Exercising
- ☐ Hiking
- ☐ Hockey
- ☐ Jogging
- ☐ Martial arts
- ☐ Sailing
- ☐ Skating
- ☐ Skiing
- ☐ Soccer
- ☐ T-Ball
- ☐ Tennis
- ☐ Tobogganing
- ☐ Observing wildlife-
- ☐ Others

____

____

Indoor Recreation

- ☐ Art-dra, paint, Cut and paste
- ☐ Nintendo,arcades Computer Games
- ☐ Crafts
- ☐ Exercising
- ☐ Friend's overnight
- ☐ Hobbies:Stamps Card collecting
- ☐ Library: Borrow Books, Reading, Research, Presentations (movies, puppet shows etc.)
- ☐ Martial arts
- ☐ Movie theatre
- ☐ Rent a movie
- ☐ Observing wildlife
- ☐ Watch TV
- ☐ Woodworking
- ☐ Others

____

____

Outdoor Recreation

- ☐ Art-draw, paint, Cut and paste
- ☐ Nintendo,Arcades Computer Games
- ☐ Baseball
- ☐ Biking
- ☐ Camping
- ☐ Card Games
- ☐ Checkers
- ☐ Chess
- ☐ Clubs: Scouting, Guiding, other
- ☐ Hiking
- ☐ Hockey
- ☐ Jogging
- ☐ Sailing
- ☐ Skating
- ☐ Skiing
- ☐ Soccer
- ☐ T-Ball
- ☐ Tennis
- ☐ Tobogganing
- ☐ Outdoor games

Phone Calls with Children

COURT TACTIX-SELF HELP
Step by Step Divorce, Separation Agreement & Parenting Guide

MONTH ________________YEAR________________

SUNDAY	MONDAY	TUESDAY	WEDNESDAY	THURSDAY	FRIDAY	SATURSDAY

Enter data from weekly phone sheets. Include any calls to or from:

- **Maternal Family**
- **Parental Family**
- **Friends (both child and either parent)**

Date Activity Cancelled	Reason Given	Re-Scheduled?

Phone Calls with Children

COURT TACTIX-SELF HELP
Step by Step Divorce, Separation Agreement & Parenting Guide

Date ____________ Start Time ____________ Finish Time ____________

Conversation with ____________ Phone Number(   ) ____________

Who initiated the call? ____________

Things we talked about ____________

Date these notes were written ____________

Signed ____________

Weekly Phone Log

COURT TACTIX-SELF HELP
Step by Step Divorce, Separation Agreement & Parenting Guide

Phone calls for the Week of Year Page No.

Time	Sunday	Monday	Tuesday	Wednesday	Thursday	Friday	Saturday
8:00 AM							
9:00 AM							
10:00 AM							
11:00 AM							
noon							
1:00 PM							
2:00 PM							
3:00 PM							
4:00 PM							
5:00 PM							
6:00 PM							
7:00 PM							
8:00 PM							
9:00 PM							
10:00 PM							
Overnight							

HIGHLIGHT DATES/TIME WHEN TELEPHONE TIMES ARE NOT POSSIBLE

Date not possible	Reason Given	Re-scheduled?

Photographs

COURT TACTIX-SELF HELP
Step by Step Divorce, Separation Agreement & Parenting Guide

A picture is worth a thousand words.

Use this space to include any photograph's taken during the month. Obtain photo mounting sheets in order to include good shots of you and your child(ren) enjoying each other's company during your parenting time. Feel free to have people assist in taking pictures, and to let your child take some photos too!

You can also turn the mounting of such photos into a fun activity where both you and the child(ren) draw some pictures for the cover of the photos, write out humorous descriptions, etc. You are only limited by your imagination.

Safety Checklist 1

COURT TACTIX-SELF HELP

Step by Step Divorce, Separation Agreement & Parenting Guide

FOR THE MONTH OF ________________YEAR________________

Use this Checklist monthly to keep your child's environment safe and secure. Most accidents are preventable if hazards are removed, safe behavior is encouraged by education. Children learn best through games- they do not realize they are learning while they are having fun, but they can understand the significance when it is illustrated to them after the game is completed. Make a game of this safety check with your child(ren). You will find they will remind you if you forget to do this, showing they can make a valuable contribution to the process. Finally, if the other parent is not safety conscious these form the basis of introducing legitimate concerns in a non-blaming manner.

CHECK THE FOLLOWING BOXES FOR EACH QUESTION: YES, NO, N/A

KITCHEN

- ☐ Discarded unused cleaning supplies?
- ☐ Locked away from children?
- ☐ Medications out of children's reach?
- ☐ Safety latches on drawers with sharp utensils?
- ☐ Safety plugs in unused outlet?
- ☐ Sturdy Step Stool to reach high cupboards?
- ☐ Non-flammable pot holders far enough away from oven/stove
- ☐ Pots & pans removed from stove after each use to prevent accidental overheating?
- ☐ Matches kept out of slight, away from heat sources, locked up?
- ☐ Adequate ventilation for kitchen area, gas ranges, to clear smoke if accident?
- ☐ Dry Chemical fire extinguisher, fully charged with Underwriters Laboratories label?
- ☐ Operating smoke detector in Kitchen?
- ☐ Appliances unplugged when not in use?
- ☐ Appliances kept far back on counter with cords out of reach of children?
- ☐
- ☐ Enough wall sockets to avoid overload a circuit?
- ☐ Do appliances have a HPN heater cord?
- ☐ Wall outlets near sinks equipped with Ground
- ☐ Fault Circuit Interrupters (To protect against electronic shocks)
- ☐ Good visibility, non glare lighting?
- ☐ Light bulbs at recommended wattage for fixtures?
- ☐ Contents in cupboards safe for kids?
- ☐ Plastic bags out of reach?
- ☐ Can table cloths be pulled by a child?
- ☐ Storage space adequate so contents do not fall out of cupboards when opened?
- ☐ Garbage container equipped with tightly fitting, secure lid? Untippable?
- ☐ Microwave positioned so kids cannot operate?
- ☐ Dishwasher unable to be opened during hot cycles?
- ☐ Are the most sharp knives locked up separately from other knives?

Parenting Schedule

COURT TACTIX-SELF HELP

Step by Step Divorce, Separation Agreement & Parenting Guide

MONTH ________________YEAR________________

SUNDAY	MONDAY	TUESDAY	WEDNESDAY	THURSDAY	FRIDAY	SATURSDAY

Dates to Remember this Month

Holidays

Easter, Hannukah

Yom Kippur

Purim, Passover

Civic Holidays

July 1st

Labor Day

Thanksgiving

Christmas

New Years

Vacations

Winter/Spring

Summer/

Long Wknds.

Special Occasions

Valentine's Day

Mother's Day

Father's Day

Graduation(s)

Sports Events

Tryouts, Recitals

School Events

Social Events

Weddings

Birthdays

Grandparents

Aunts/Uncles

Mother/Father

In-Laws

Sister/Brother

Children

Step-relatives

Other Relatives

Friends

Parenting Letters

COURT TACTIX-SELF HELP

Step by Step Divorce, Separation Agreement & Parenting Guide

Letters to your children: Copies of letters to your child(ren) should be included here. Your letters should be playful and fun to read and explore. There are many techniques to writing a fun letter to a child. These can include creating games such as: guessing games, puzzles, crosswords, stories, pictures, fill in the blank games. Including small items such as special pencils and erasers for writing back to the parent who sent the letter will be appreciated also. Remember, the very best parenting letters are one where it is a game that the child can play with the parent and send back for the parent to take their turn, make their move etc.

Letters to the other parent: Copies of letters to the other parent should be included here. These can prove difficult if communication is at an all time low. Be concise, co-operative and conciliatory. Confrontational letters serve no one's best interests. Above all, be pleasant! Good letters are focused on the subject matter; they avoid inflammatory remarks, do not seek to place blame, or attempt to make the other parent be what the parent writing the letter wants them to be. *Have an unbiased party review your letters and offer suggestions.*

Letters to the other parent's family: Copies of letters to the other parent's family should be included here. These letters can be effective in reducing family tensions if done well and following the guidelines above. The rule of thumb should be forgiveness and guarantees of non-interference with access to the kids. Inflammatory language must be avoided in such letters.

Letters to the 3rd parties: Letters to 3rd parties such as schools, doctor's, those involved with the divorce such as Assessors, social workers, court clerks, etc., should also be concise, co-operative and conciliatory. Confrontational letters serve no one's best interests. Be Pleasant! For those needing guidelines for what constitutes good letter writing during divorce please refer to our publication: "Parenting Letters: An Effective Tool During Divorce"

Phone Calls

COURT TACTIX-SELF HELP
Step by Step Divorce, Separation Agreement & Parenting Guide

Date Start Time Finish Time

Conversation with Phone Number

Who initiated the call?

Things we talked about

Date these notes were written

Signed

Incident Report

COURT TACTIX-SELF HELP
Step by Step Divorce, Separation Agreement & Parenting Guide

Date Start Time Page No.

What happened?

Where did it happen?

Who was there?

Why did it happen?

What's the next move?

Solution

Missing 107, 108, 109, 110

Incident Report

Date	Action Taken	Response

Conclusion

This book is intended only as an insight into how to conduct a simple divorce proceeding of the most common kind. It is not intended to be specific to any one jurisdiction. It is not supposed to be an in-depth treatment of any one topic. It is a guideline with suggestions about how to get your point across and how to achieve your goal.

Naturally there is much more that could be said. There are many known variations and combinations in human relationships and circumstances. We cannot hope to cover them all or solve the specific problems of all readers. If answers to specific or complex questions are needed, there are many community legal advice clinics and low cost legal aid referral services available in most communities throughout North America.

We have made certain editorial decisions for the sake of brevity and clarity. This has meant that certain topics of somewhat greater complexity have been omitted.

For example, in a work such as this, dealing primarily with uncontested divorce, there is no way to reduce the many broad and complicated aspects of interim (temporary) support, custody and access for visits to a manageable size and level of simplicity that lay readers could handle. Interim support, custody and access are frequently occurring issues, but usually in hotly contested cases and usually as emergency motions.

Similarly the subjects of child custody and access visits and support, both spousal and child support are big enough that entire books have been written focusing just on these parts of family law alone. They are big subjects, broad and complex and are often the sources of bitter disputes between parties in divorce proceedings.

If you have a relatively high degree of spousal co-operation, if your goals are modest and straightforward and you can relatively expect to achieve them or you are learning how the legal system works in a divorce situation, or if you like being informed and having a benchmark against which to measure what you see and hear, perhaps from your own lawyer, then we hope you have recognized in these pages some of yourself and your situation.

If we have made even one solution seem within reach for one person, then we have helped to improve that one life – for that reason this book was worth the effort.

Printed in the USA
CPSIA information can be obtained
at www.ICGtesting.com
LVHW080752200624
783559LV00031B/550

9 781956 096675